FOUNDATIONS OF FAITH

❧

HISTORIC RELIGIOUS BUILDINGS OF ONTARIO

Happy Reading!

Violet M. Holrayd

FOUNDATIONS OF FAITH

ぇ

HISTORIC RELIGIOUS BUILDINGS OF ONTARIO

VIOLET M. HOLROYD

NATURAL HERITAGE /NATURAL HISTORY INC.

Canadian Cataloguing in Publication Data
Holroyd, Violet M.
    Foundations of faith: historic religious buildings of Ontario

Includes bibliographical references and index.
ISBN 0-920474-64-0

1. Church architecture – Ontario. 2. Ontario – Religious and ecclesiastical institutions – Guide-books. 3. Historic buildings – Ontario – Guide-books. I. Title

NA5246.O5H6 1991   726'.09713   C91-094842-9

The publisher gratefully acknowledges the support of the Ontario Arts Council.

Design: Molly Brass

Printed and bound in Canada by Hignell Printing Limited

I dedicate this book to my husband
Gordon Arthur Holroyd
without whose help and understanding
it could not have been written

CONTENTS

FOREWORD

Ontario, not unlike other provinces of Canada, is a land of immigrants. Wherever the pioneers and later immigrants settled, they brought with them "the Faith of their Fathers".

Throughout rural and urban Ontario, spires tall and small point the people to God. There is not a hamlet without a House of Worship and there is not a community without its Church Street.

In this work, Violet Holroyd has relived for us the local history of many of the places of worship in our province. She further portrays for us how the people built their temples of faith.

These historic buildings are memorials to the determination and hardship of the pioneers who found strength, guidance and comfort in the message of these meeting places. It was they who laid the foundations, visible and invisible, upon which the moral fibre of the province was built.

This book, well researched, and written in a very readable style, is a work that should be in the collection of every local history library in the province of Ontario.

(REV.) F. ALLEN PICKERING

PREFACE

This is neither a religious book nor a history book but a resource guide featuring some of the fascinating stories behind some of Ontario's oldest places of worship.

In the writing of it, I have travelled the length and breadth of our province to personally visit these sites. Regrettably it is impossible to include all of the rich variety of religious centres. In making the selection for my book, emphasis has been placed on historical sites and accessibility for the traveller and personal favourites.

Every effort has been made to authenticate names, dates, places and other historical facts. The information was gained primarily from personal observation and from interviews and correspondence with the many persons listed in the acknowledgements. My heartfelt thanks goes to all who helped in this project.

It is my hope that you will travel this beautiful province and visit some of these historic buildings.

THE AUTHOR

ACKNOWLEDGEMENTS

James Bay Frontier, Timmins, Ontario; The Right Reverend Caleb J. Lawrence, B.A., B.S.T., D.D., Bishop of Moosonee; Miss Grace Procunier, Etobicoke, Ontario; Fr. Donald A. Tuori, Pakenham, Ontario; Fr. Cylinzki, Wilno, Ontario; The Rev. Canon R.H. Stewart, B.A., B.D., Prescott, Ontario; Edwin A. Livingston, C.D., U.E., Prescott, Ontario; Mr. James B. Maracle, Deseronto, Ontario; Mr. John Nalon, President Gananoque Historical Society, Gananóoque, Ontario; Rev. William Lamb, Etobicoke, Ontario; Rev. John A. Read, B.A., M.Div., Port Hope, Ontario; Canon D. Ralph Spence, Burlington, Ontario; Mrs. Gladys R. Zimmerman, Brantford, Ontario; Mr. Arthur Pegg, County of Kent Historic Advisor/Director, Uncle Tom's Cabin Historic Site, Dresden, Ontario; Ms. Darlene Carter, Dresden, Ontario; Mrs. Earl Hunt, Mount Forest, Ontario; Sr. Linda Gregg, Pastoral Minister, Immaculate Conception Church,, West Bay, Ontario; Rev. David R. Burrows, Bobcaygeon, Ontario; Central Ontario Travel Association, Peterborough, Ontario; The Rev. Richard Miller, Shanty Bay, Ontario; Rev. Jeffrey E. Smith, M.Div., Leaskdale, Ontario; Rev. William Ray, Uxbridge, Ontario; S. Klassen, Elora, Ontario; Rev. Robert Hulse, Elora, Ontario; Mr. Robert B. King, Eden Mills, Ontario; Ms. Barbara Smiley, Rockwood, Ontario; Rev. Monsignor John Newstead, Guelph, Ontario; Mrs. Lorraine O'Byrne, Assistant Curator, Black Creek Pioneer Village; James J. Farrell, Director, Martyrs' Shrine, Midland, Ontario; Mr. William Elliott, Etobicoke, Ontario; Mr. Isaac Horst, Mount Forest, Ontario; Miss Lillian Loucks, Keene, Ontario; Miss Judith St. John, Willowdale, Ontario; Stephen A. Speisman, M.A., Ph.D., Toronto Jewish Congress Archives; T.

McDonald, Alliston, Ontario; Ms. Mary Perriman, Ayr, Ontario; Mrs. Margaret Deans, Paris, Ontario; Mary-Anne Mihorean, Archivist, The Anglican Diocese of Toronto; Dorothy Kesley, Assistant Archivist, The Anglican Diocese of Toronto; Rev. G. Ferris, Paris, Ontario; Mr. Harry Husbins, Archivist, Diocese of Algoma, Sault Ste. Marie, Ontario: Patricia Rucker, Leila Speisman, Canadian Jewish News; Wayne Tanenbaum; Edwin Goldstein, President, Knesseth Israel Synanogue

Photography Credits

The Gananoque Historical Society, Gananoque, Ontario; Church of Our Lady, Guelph; Toronto Jewish Congress/Canadian Jewish Congress, Ontario Region Archives, Toronto, Ontario
All other photography, Sidney Holroyd, Etobicoke, Ontario

FOUNDATIONS OF FAITH

HISTORIC RELIGIOUS BUILDINGS OF ONTARIO

St. Thomas Church

ANGLICAN ✤ MOOSE FACTORY

Set your compass on Adventure! Board the Polar Bear Express at Cochrane, Ontario. Sit back and watch the wilderness unfold as you parallel the river routes and paths of native Canadians, explorers, fur traders and prospectors north two hundred and ninety-seven kilometres to Moosonee. You've come to the rail's end and the start of fresh adventure.

The three kilometre journey via a giant Rupert House canoe brings you to Moose Factory Island, one of the two oldest settlements in Ontario and the first English speaking of the two.

The town of Moose Factory was founded in 1673 by the Hudson's Bay Company. For nearly two centuries it remained a frontier trading post, sheltering explorers, adventurers and pioneers against the rigors of the north.

Now it is a beautiful thriving tourist attraction with a population of over two thousand. Although quite modern in many respects, there is a feeling of timelessness as though history stood still waiting for us to catch up with it. This can be felt in the few original buildings still standing but in none more pronounced than inside the old historic church.

The Polar Bear Express and a giant canoe takes you to the fringes of the true north of Ontario, to St. Thomas Church, Moose Factory.

St. Thomas Anglican Church is probably the most unique of all Ontario churches, old or new. Built in 1860, it has been wonderfully cared for. In years past, ice coming down the river would snag on the sandbars around the island and pile up, creating a massive natural dam. Eventually, the ice, pressured by the water back-up, would give way with a tremendous roar and avalanche downstream, sweeping everything before it.

On one such occasion, the church sailed away on the flood waters. Fortunately, the people managed to tow it back into place before the water went down. The memory of the event gave rise to the oft repeated myth, "To prevent this from happening again, holes were bored in the floor and fitted with wooden plugs. In case of a flood, the holes could be unplugged and water allowed to enter the church thus preventing it from floating away". Actually, the plugs in the floor were part of the original construction of the building. They were meant to be removed each spring *to allow the water from the snow and ice melt to evaporate*. Failure to follow this intended practise, probably due to the influence of the myth cited above, led to the eventual rot of the entire building foundation which was eventually replaced with concrete, but at considerable cost.

Like most other churches, the women, most of whom were native Cree Indians, played a prominent role. They gave of their time and talents to make the beautiful moose-hide hangings which adorn the altar, indeed a labour of love. They were painstakingly executed with coloured beadwork showing the birds and animals of the area. The women gather in the adjacent parish hall to serve lunches to tourists and sell native handcrafts.

Inside the church, Bibles and Hymnals, well-worn books printed in both the Cree and English Languages, are arranged on shelves at the entrance. In the nearby original churchyard, weathered tombstones with stories and epitaphs, many carved in the Cree language, mark the graves of the rugged fur-trading pioneers and those whom they met and with whom they shared life's adventures.

St. Thomas' Church is just one more example of man's unquenchable desire to worship his God wherever he happens to be and in whatever way he wishes.

ST. PETER CELESTINE

ROMAN CATHOLIC ❧ PAKENHAM

T he peaceful little village of Pakenham in the picturesque Ottawa Valley is the home of one of Canada's most beautiful churches.

When Peter Robinson's Irish immigrants arrived in the area in 1823, there was no Roman Catholic Church. They suffered many privations and hardships but, in spite of their condition, they settled in and built a town. In time a small frame church was built and services were held through those early years by travelling missionaries.

In 1876, Father D. Lavin started a fund towards the building of a new church. Eighteen thousand dollars was raised by 1892 when the cornerstone was laid for the present church. People came from every direction in carriages of all description, on horseback or on foot for the consecration in 1898 of The Church of St. Peter Celestine.

This splendid church of Gothic architecture stands imposingly on a hill, known locally as Piety Hill, in a lovely setting framed by tall maples and spruce. The village lies below in the shadow of the cross and for many miles the shining silvered steeple and spire are seen towering heavenward. The bells ring out the Angelus at morning, noon and evening to remind us to halt briefly

Peter Robinson, Irish immigrant in 1823, would be astonished at the sight of the beautiful Church of St. Peter Celestine on "Piety Hill" in Pakenham.

in our busy lives for prayer and spiritual reflection. They toll at the death of a parishioner and have, on occasion, been used as fire alarms.

The church is one hundred and thirty feet by sixty-five feet, the walls thirty feet high on a foundation five feet thick. The spire is one hundred and thirty-nine feet from the ground and is surmounted by a cross. The twelve foot statue of Christ over the main entrance is plated in gold and was cast in France. The entire building is sheeted with the best galvanized iron, put on by Mr. John Knox, a skilled workman employed by an Arnprior contractor.

The splendour of St. Peter Celestine's interior is breathtaking. A special feature, when you enter, is its height — no pillars. The altar, statuary and stained-glass windows are outstanding works of art.

Perhaps the largest gathering of people ever to be seen in the area was on the laying of the cornerstone on July 31, 1892. Two to three thousand attended the ceremony where a pulpit and altar surrounded by evergreens decked with white roses had been erected. An hermetically sealed casket containing records of the event, newspaper accounts, etc. was placed in the cavity and the stone was laid with a solid silver trowel.

After the sermon, everyone was invited to go forward and strike the stone, reminding them at the same time that they would be expected to contribute something. The collection, liberal for the times, amounted to one thousand and three dollars.

The multitudes, in good humour for their dinner, rushed to the hotels. The demands were so great that the cooks were unable to keep up. Many got half a meal or none at all. Nevertheless, it was a fantastic day in the life of such a small town. It was early evening when the "Soo" train steamed westward from Pakenham carrying with it the last of the visitors.

When the church was completed on December 17, 1893, the tolling of the bell summoned worshippers for the last time to the old church where low mass was celebrated. It was an emotional time for many people. After the mass, the congregation proceeded to the new edifice where first the exterior, then the interior were blessed.

The Church of St. Peter Celestine has played a noble part in the community's history. It is significant of the fine sense of spiritual values which inspired our forebears, whose tradition of godliness and neighbourly love continues today.

ST. MARY'S ROMAN CATHOLIC CHURCH

WILNO

Travel east of Barry's Bay on highway 60, near the small town of Wilno, Ontario, and you will see the magnificent Shrine Hill lookout. Be prepared to walk up many steps to St. Mary's Roman Catholic Church where you can look out over the Wilno hills between the Madawaska and Ottawa valleys.

The region was first inhabited by the Algonquin Indians with whom the French explorers and traders developed an active fur trade and later engaged in the timber industry. Then came the Irish settlers, followed by the Scots, after whom the Poles arrived and established the village of Wilno.

The Government of Upper Canada was determined that the region be turned into an agricultural area and offered the settlers free grants of fifty acres with an option of an additional fifty acres later. It was the promise of free land that attracted the Polish Kashoubs in the late 1850's. The opportunity came at a time when they were being persecuted by the Prussians in their homeland. They were full of hope as they made their perilous journey across the Atlantic. Many died during the crossing and were buried at sea.

Life in their new land was far from easy. Many were illiterate; a lack of forest clearing equipment and an inability to communicate with their Irish and Scottish neighbours made "togetherness" a permanent factor in the struggle for survival. In time, economic conditions improved and life in general became a little better for everyone.

In 1872, a Polish priest arrived in Wilno. He lasted only a short time and was followed by several others, during which time a small log church was built in 1875. Finally, in 1892, Father Bronislaw Jankowski arrived in Wilno and gave new life to the community. He spent many years encouraging more immigrants and building up the Parish. The little church was called St. Stanislaus and was finally finished and dedicated in 1895. New immigrants swelled the number of Poles to twenty-five hundred and the parish thrived.

The town of Wilno is called the Polish Capital of Canada. Polish immigrants started the congregation of St. Mary's in a log cabin.

Unfortunately, in 1936, the old wooden church, built with so much effort and sacrifice, burned to the ground. The parishioners began at once to build a new church and by Christmas of the following year, the church was ready, all the work having been done without pay by some sixty parishioners. It was named Our Lady, Queen of Poland, and is the most impressive building in the valley.

In 1939, the Polish Consul in Canada presented a copy of the painting of Our Lady of Czestochowa to the church on behalf of President Ignacy Moscicki of Poland.

On the occasion of St. Mary's one hundred year anniversary the Honourable William Davis, who was Premier of Ontario at the time, attended a special service to present the church with a diploma. It read as follows: *"From the Canadian Polish Congress. To all to whom these presents shall come or whom the same may anywise concern, we hereby declare to be known and certify that in the year of the 100th Anniversary of the founding of the first Polish Roman Catholic Church in Wilno, Ontario, and in honour of the great contribution of the parish in preserving the Polish culture and faith among its parishioners, we grant this diploma to St. Mary's Parish in Wilno, Ontario, June 21, 1975"*.

The beautiful stained glass windows cast a radiant glow throughout the interior of the church. New sculptures were added to the old in three phases in the years 1985, 1986 and 1987.

The Polish community in Wilno, as in other Polish communities in Canada, is predominantly of a religious rather than a secular nature. The church is also the place where social activities are held. Though conscious of their roots, new generations are evolving from the closeknit community of yesterday, taking part in all phases of civic, cultural and social activities and are found in almost every area of national life.

Canada owes a great deal to the settlers from all countries who have made this their home. Ontario is especially grateful to the Polish immigrants who built this great edifice and who have added their culture to the other cultures that make up the social fabric of our province.

THE BLUE CHURCH

ANGLICAN ❧ PRESCOTT

After the American Revolutionary War, thousands of United Empire Loyalists and discharged British soldiers were granted land along the St. Lawrence River westward from Cornwall to the mouth of the Gananoque River.

One of those settlers, Captain Justus Sherwood, became a surveyor and aided in the laying out of townships in the area. A town site with six streets running east and west and four streets running north and south was laid out in 1784. Space was allotted to the church commons, the land now occupied by the Blue Church and the burying ground. The town, however, which was to be called "New Oswegatchie" never amounted to anything. Most of the settlers preferred to stay on larger tracts of land where they could farm, and for sixteen years the church commons was used only as a burying ground.

In 1790 citizens agreed that a church should be built there. Subscription lists were drawn up, but the sponsors failed to get enough funds to erect a church. Even so, the pioneers were not without religious services. Barbara Heck, known as the mother of Methodism in Canada along with her husband Paul, organized ser-

This pretty little Blue Church on Highway #2 near Prescott is the colour of an Ontario summer sky. It is the scene of many picturesque weddings in summer.

vices to be held in private homes, the log cabins of the settlers. The Methodist "Circuit Riders" kept alive the spirit of religious life and made life more bearable for the settlers in view of the hardships they suffered in those days.

Sometime between 1794 and 1814, the first Blue Church was built on the burying ground. In the early 1840's fire broke out, resulting in such damage that the church had to be torn down. The congregation got together and built a new church which opened in 1845. This is the Blue Church standing today on the north side of Highway Two.

It began as an Anglican house of worship and remains so today. A monument to Barbara Heck was erected in a plot assigned to the Methodist Church of Canada. The legend inscribed thereon states: "In memory of one who laid foundations others have built upon. Barbara Heck put her brave soul against the rugged possibilities of the future and under God brought into existence American and Canadian Methodism and between those, her memory will ever form a most hallowed link".

This tiny church, not much larger than most living rooms, with room for only two windows on each side, makes a charming picture among the well-kept lawns and old gravestones. The interior is about as plain as you will find anywhere. Rough wooden pews and other primitive furnishings keep one in touch with the past. The clapboard exterior has always been blue and is kept freshly painted the colour of sky on a bright summer day.

The church is open from May until after Thanksgiving each year. Bus tours, church groups and many individual visitors sign the guest book. Many picturesque weddings take place there and a special anniversary service is held each year on the third Sunday in June at 2:00 P.M.

Although the village of New Oswegatchie and the days of the United Empire Loyalists have faded into the dim distant days of old, the lovely Blue Church remains, the only reminder in that area of glories past.

CHRIST CHURCH

ANGLICAN ❧ TYENDINAGA

I n 1710, four Chiefs of the Five Nations Confederacy from the Mohawk Valley in New York State visited England. They were conveyed to St. James Palace in Royal Coaches for an audience with Queen Anne.

Through an interpreter they asked that a missionary be sent to teach their people the ways of Christianity. The request was granted and construction of a chapel was begun in 1711. As well, the Queen sent a communion table, altar cloths, carpet, prayer books, a Bible and a fine silver communion service. The silver, two flagons, two chalices, two patens and an alms basin were of higher purity than sterling.

During the American Revolution, the silver was buried for safety. When the war ended, the members of the Six Nations who had remained loyal to the British Crown had to leave the Mohawk Valley. Some of them, under Joseph Brant, settled near Brantford. The others, under John Deserontyou, chose the Bay of Quinte. In 1784 a party was dispatched to the Mohawk Valley. They secretly dug up the silver and brought it to Canada where it was divided between the two bands. The silver pieces, with the exception of one chalice which was lost, are kept in Christ Church, Tyendinaga In-

Every year on the 24th of May holiday weekend, Christ Church, Tyendinaga, and the surrounding area is the setting for the reenactment of the landing of the Mohawks, an intriguing journey back into history.

dian Reserve, Deseronto, Ontario, and are used at least three times a year — Christmas, Easter and Mohawk Sunday.

Christ Church is officially one of six British Royal Chapels in the world. It has been long known to the Tyendinaga Mohawks that the chapel was actually designated as a Royal Chapel in 1798 when King George III gave the church a bell, a Royal Coat of Arms and a triptych.

The first Christ Church was built in 1784. It was a quaint little log building with seats made of rounds of large tree trunks about two feet high. The door was frame, covered with a deer skin in an intricately wrought design. It had a latch on the inside only. The church, although it had no belfry, had a bell which hung on poles outside.

That first primitive house of worship was replaced in 1843 by the present Christ Church. Its limestone blocks were lovingly and labouriously hand cut by the native people. It was partially destroyed by fire in 1906 and rebuilt in 1907 into a particularly fine stone structure with a Gothic tower. At that time, the bell which had originated in England in 1778, was shipped back there to be recast by the same company which had made it, John Warner and Sons.

Surrounded by tall elm and hickory trees, it stands high on a hill overlooking the Bay of Quinte. It is a sacred museum of irreplaceable mememtos of the proud Mohawk band and its loyalty to Britain.

Over the altar is the triptych given by King George III. It contains the Creed, the Ten Commandments and the Lord's Prayer, all written in the Mohawk Language. The magnificent altar cross is a work of art, inlaid mother-of-pearl on olive wood from the Mount of Olives. It was brought from Jerusalem by the daughter of Dr. Oronhyatekha, the famed Indian doctor who revamped and saved from bankruptcy the world-wide organization of the Independant Order of Foresters. The doctor was a renowned Mohawk Chief, orator and physician, born on the Grand River Reservation. He attended the University of Toronto and Oxford and, at the age of twenty, was selected by the six Nations to present official greetings to the visiting Prince of Wales. In 1871, he was a member of Canada's first Wembleton Rifle Team and, in 1874, became President of the Grand Council of Canadian Chiefs. He died in 1907 and is buried in the churchyard. The altar desk is also made of olive wood from Jerusalem.

In 1984, on the occasion of Christ Church's bicentennial, Queen Elizabeth and Prince Philip visited the church. The Queen unveiled a beautiful stained-glass window and presented a new original chalice to her Royal Chapel to replace the one lost many years before. The cup is decorated with stylized pine trees, each topped with an eagle. The stem is the Tree of Peace with its roots spreading over the base which includes a turtle, wolf and bear, each symbolizing the three Mohawk clans.

The silver for the chalice was mined in Ontario. It bears the inscription: "The gift of Her Majesty the Queen to her Mohawk Chapel, Christ Church, Bay of Quinte, 1984". The chalice is kept with the famous Queen Anne communion service.

In one corner of the church a glass case holds a large-print Bible, the gift of Queen Victoria in 1842. Unfortunately it was not signed at that time. In 1951, when our Queen was Princess Elizabeth, she came with Prince Philip and added the Royal Signature.

In another corner stands a wooden box containing a piece of the limestone from the original Queen Anne Chapel in New York State. The Baptismal Font near it is over one hundred years old.

During the long weekend in May each year the town of Deseronto takes on a festive air. A re-enactment of the landing of the Mohawks takes place in full Indian dress, dancing and all the trimmings. On the Sunday, a special commemorative service is held in Christ Church.

Today, this beautiful old stone church is a repository of emblematic links with the Crown, with enough signs of royal affection to make even the loyalest of United Empire Loyalists look like plebians.

HALF MOON BAY

NON-DENOMINATIONAL ❧ GANANOQUE

Ontario has many beautiful tourist attractions. Visitors from all over Canada and the United States come to enjoy our Thousand Islands. One of the islands has a little more to offer than the others.

Bostwick Island is situated approximately one and a half miles from the town of Gananoque. On the southeast end of the island is a small crescent-shaped inlet known as Half Moon Bay. A unique geological formation, it was created in a rushing torrent of water perhaps as long ago as a half million years. Water poured over the island and under great pressure shot through a cut at the end of the bay. One of the extraordinary features created were the deep pot-holes. these were carved by the whirling eddies and are located at the west end of the bay.

Over one hundred years ago, in 1887, a group of summer campers discovered this quiet secluded place and began holding divine services. They came in boats, the only access to the island. Rowboats, small skiffs and canoes anchored in the bay to hear men of various denominations preach from a rock pulpit on the shore. Later, boats with one or two-cylinder engines, which often had to be cranked, began appearing. The people sat upright in their boats, dressed in their Sunday best, high collars and straw hats.

Wood gave way to fibreglass and metal. Today's congregation is made up of people in their casual summer clothes, lounging in outboards, houseboats and yachts. Although the trees and cliffs remain largely unchanged, the all-granite pulpit has been moved from its original position to a higher location. The stone pier has given way to a concrete one. Yet despite the change in dress and mode of transportation, participation in this outdoor service continues to be popular with area cottagers.

You'll need a boat to get to the Half Moon Bay Rock Pulpit, and bring an umbrella in case of rain.

Half Moon Bay vespers have been attracting worshippers for over a hundred years for meditation, prayer and hymns. Today, as then, services are held every Sunday during July and August beginning at 5:00 P.M. Local ministers and laymen from Canada, United States and abroad hold interdenominational services.

In this small natural amphitheatre no steeple points skyward. There is no church, no choir loft, no carpeted aisle. The sun does not shine through stained-glass windows but through the gently waving, sun-dappled branches of trees, on the sparkling waters of the bay and on the rough rock pulpit. But that does not matter because, in the long run, the *church is people*.

THE WHITE CHAPEL

EARLY LOYALIST METHODIST ❧ PICTON

T he White Chapel, a picture of serenity, stands among large shade trees and old tombstones on Highway 49, five kilometres north east of Picton.

An early Loyalist Methodist meeting house, built in 1809, it is one of the few examples of Loyalist architecture left in the country. It is beautifully preserved and is open to the public during the summer. Reminiscent of ecclesiastical buildings in 17th century New England, the Chapel is a vivid testimony to the country's Loyalist roots.

Before the chapel was built, Methodist Episcopal ministers travelled from homestead to homestead bringing religion to the settlers. Then, willing workers felled the trees and squared the timbers. Others with oxen and horses drew the hewed pieces to the chosen place. There the building was framed and a bee was organized. It was a great day when all the settlers and their families gathered for the "raising". Begun in June of 1809, it was finished in 1811. The master carpenter was William Moore who had been an engineer for the British Army in the American Revolutionary War before coming to the Bay of Quinte area with the Associated Loyalists.

The White Chapel was more finished than others in the area. It's windows had glass and sash. You can still see some of the wavy panes which tell you just how old the building is. It's exterior had siding and was painted white. The inside fixtures were painted and part of the interior had wallpaper.

The land upon which the church stands was donated by Stephen Conger, the ninth son of one of the earlier settlers who came in the 1700's. In the well-kept graveyard are tomb-stones marking the burial places of the pioneers. The names and dates are barely distinguishable, washed and worn by years of storm and sun. A few of the markers are wood. Lovingly carved and placed there by families who could not afford stones, they are now bleached almost white and parts of them have rotted away.

The White Chapel is now owned by the United Church of Canada and is maintained by a Board of Governors appointed by

The White Chapel, Picton, is open only one Sunday in June for a service commemorating the United Empire Loyalist Methodists.

the Picton United Church. When compared to that beautiful, massive, stone church, the little chapel may seem insignificant, but it has been maintained as a place of worship for a longer time than any other church of Methodist origin in Ontario and is still the site of an annual commemoration service in June.

The White Chapel stands today as a tribute to the pioneer days and to the Methodist saddle-bag preachers who preached their sermons and formed a way of life; a tradition which is far greater than their own religious denomination and out of which the United Church of Canada evolved.

THE HAY BAY CHURCH

METHODIST EPISCOPAL ❧ BAY OF QUINTE

The old Hay Bay Church, first built in 1792 by members of the Methodist Episcopal Church, stands on the south shore of Hay Bay which empties into the picturesque Bay of Quinte in Eastern Ontario. It was the first church erected by Methodists west of the Maritimes and is the oldest building belonging to the United Church of Canada. It has been preserved as by a miracle and stands today as witness to the devoted labours of our fathers and a symbol of their faith and ours.

One of the consequences of the American Revolution was a veritable invasion by about forty thousand persons, mostly English-speaking and Protestant, who preferred to live under the government of Great Britain. A number of these, United Empire Loyalists as they were called, eventually made their way from the north eastern states, New York, New Jersey and Pennsylvania. They came in boatloads up through Quebec from New York City and west along the St. Lawrence River to the Bay of Quinte area. Each family was provided with a tent, some clothing, implements and tools and a cow, and was to receive help from the Government for three years. They endured severe hardships and privation for several years.

In 1788, one of the settlers, a young teacher and licensed Exhorter of the Methodist Episcopal Church, began teaching and conducting services in homes throughout the area. No one knows for sure what happened to him but it appears his stay was short. It is thought that he was ridiculed for his Methodism and that his school was boycotted. Likely, he returned from whence he came.

That same year, Mr. McCarty came to preach, not to settle, and he, too, was not welcome. He was arrested as a "vagabond" and asked to leave. He did so but returned only to be sent to jail until a proper conveyance could be found to escort him out of the country. The tradition is that he was murdered but the evidence is far from conclusive.

Now the oldest church building belonging to the United Church in Canada, Hay Bay Church is the scene of an annual pilgrimage on the last Sunday in August.

It wasn't until 1789 that an ordained Methodist preacher came to the province. William Losee arrived and stirred the people with his dynamic preaching. Under his leadership, scores of willing hands resorted to the woods to fell the trees and square the timbers. Others with oxen and horses drew the pieces to the building site where the frames were constructed. At last, a "bee" was called to raise the building, after which it was enclosed, windows and doors were put in and a rough floor laid.

The finished structure, Hay Bay Church, was thirty-six feet by thirty feet, two storeys high with a gallery on the second storey. Constructed of white pine, the timbers were fastened together by mortise and tenon joints, held tight with driven-in wooden pegs. No metal nails or spikes were used. Nails of the 1790's were hand-wrought by a blacksmith or his apprentice. They were a valuable commodity and were used only to apply flooring, siding and shingles. The floor planks were tongue and groove pine. Roof shingles were hand-split cedar.

The pulpit, reached by stairs, was built high enough so that the "preacher" could address those in the gallery as well as those below. Above the pulpit was the sounding board, designed to improve the acoustics and typical of that period.

The gallery floor was built with a nine degree slope instead of the step-like tiers evident in other church galleries. The original seating there was rough planks on stumps and a few homemade efforts at more comfortable seats. More "modern" pews with backs on them were added in the early 1800's, and these are the style in the church at the present time.

The building was used immediately for preaching, prayer meetings, quarterly meetings and sometimes, over the years, as a courthouse or municipal building. During the War of 1812-1814, the church was even used as a barracks and, for some time, the Good Templars' Lodge held its meetings there.

The congregation increased and the building began to deteriorate making enlargement and reconstruction necessary in 1835. The size was increased by one-third and the roof turned around so that the long axis of the roof, instead of extending east and west, extended north and south.

The church was used for twenty-five years and then, partly due to a shift in the population and partly no doubt to the need for more extensive repairs, was abandoned. It stood almost in the waters of Hay Bay, silent and alone, hoary with years, yet stately in its ruin, even though the pulpit seats and altar were gone. It was sold to Percival Platt for fifty dollars. The congregation built a new church one concession south.

Finally, in 1910, through the efforts of Mr. Allan Ross Davis, a descendant of one of the subscribers to the building fund of the original church, and Chancellor Nathaniel Burwash of Victoria College, the church and graveyard were re-purchased for the Methodist Church for three hundred dollars.

Restoration began again and, in the years that followed, furnishings of the same period (circa late 1700's and early 1800's) were found. The flag pole attached to the rear of the church flies the British Union Flag which did not have the red diagonal cross of St. Patrick on it until the union with Ireland in 1801.

When Church Union came in 1925, the Hay Bay Church became the property of the United Church of Canada. Regular restoration and conservation continues to this day. The Board of Trustees has arranged an annual pilgrimage to the church on the fourth Sunday of August when an appropriate service is held. Some three thousand pilgrims and tourists visit it every summer.

In 1892, the centennial of Hay Bay Church, a man named Richard Duke wrote: "Hay Bay Church links us visibly with the rise of Methodism in Ontario...and is the embodiment of a hundred years of our history as a distinct people in this land". Then, in 1924, a Dr. Chown said, "The church that forgets its past deserves no future".

Hay Bay Church will not let us forget.

St. Peter's Church

ANGLICAN ❧ COBOURG

Early in the 19th century, it was probable that the Society for the Propagation of the Gospel visited the area around Cobourg. However, when the town itself was founded in 1819, a young priest was sent by the Bishop of Quebec to minister to the spiritual needs of the town settlers.

The first services were held in a wooden building that then served both as Court House and Jail. As a temporary place of worship, it sufficed but the people wanted a church. In 1820, they got busy and built one on the site of the present church of St. Peter. That first St. Peter's Church was a simple wooden structure measuring fifty-six by forty-four feet. It wasn't long before the congregation outgrew it. It was enlarged in 1829 and, in 1844, a tower and spire were added.

By the middle of the 1800's the population of Cobourg and the surrounding area had greatly increased and it was clear that an even larger church was needed.

Kivas Tully, a well-known architect at that time who later built Victoria Hall was given the job. The new church, built in Early Gothic Revival style, was constructed *around* the existing one. In the last stages, the old building was taken apart and carried

St. Peter's Church, Cobourg, was built around the old existing church. In the last stages, the old building was taken apart and carried out through the front door piece by piece.

out through the front doors piece by piece. While that was being done, services were held in the malt room of the local brewery. The new church was completed in 1854.

Further increases in the congregation made necessary a permanent home for the Sunday School. Thus, in 1891, another building was erected on church property, reasonably close to the church.

Many beautiful memorial stained-glass windows and pieces of furniture were given during the years following. Then, in 1927, the Sunday School building and the Church were joined by a memorial tower which contained a Guild Room, kitchen, gymnasium, and office and one other room that was used as a men's club until 1957, when it was transformed into a small chapel. It is beautifully appointed, radiating peace and serenity when you enter. The stained-glass windows depict the life of Paul, and so it was named the Chapel of St. Paul. Thus, St. Peter and St. Paul, the two greatest of the apostles, were linked in this parish.

The windows in the narthex were originally in the Mortuary Chapel in St. Peter's Cemetery. When the mortuary Chapel was no longer in use, the windows were painstakingly removed and placed in the narthex. They are invaluable in that the work embodied in them can no longer be reproduced.

A chime of ten bells operated by a keyboard of wooden levers struck by hand, was dedicated on May 7, 1905, and hangs in the tower above the narthex. The chime was restored and rededicated in 1980 at a special service at which Mr. Gordon Slater, Dominion Carillioneur (Peace Tower, Ottawa) was recitalist.

One of the modern touches added to the church are the doors opening into the main body of the church. They are plate glass with handles in the shape of fish, a symbol of Christ in Christian art and literature.

The manner in which St. Peter's church has been kept in a continual state of repair and renovation by dedicated congregations has made this beautiful church "A legacy to those who come from those who come no more".

St. Mark's Church & St. John the Evangelist

ANGLICAN ❧ PORT HOPE

T he history of St. John's Church on Pine Street in Port Hope would not be complete without the story of St. Mark's Church.

Situated on the east side of the Ganaraska River, St. Mark's Church gleams white in the sunshine. This beautiful little Gothic Style clapboard building has a square steeple topped with a minaret that resembles the turret of a small castle. Begun in 1822 and completed in 1824, it was smaller then than now. It is recorded that the Rector from Cobourg, in order to carry out his duties, travelled by horse, wagon, sleigh or boat, depending on the season.

The church was consecrated in 1828 and dedicated to St. John the Evangelist. It was enlarged in 1842, and alterations to the windows and tower were made in 1851. It served the Anglican congregation until its closure in 1869.

By that time, most of the population of Port Hope had settled on the *west* bank of the Ganaraska River, so the decision was made to build a new church there. A lot was purchased for $1800.00 dollars and construction began seventeen days after Confederation.

The building was completed in 1869 at a total cost of $18,300.00 dollars and opened just as the former St. Mark's church closed.

The new St. John the Evangelist, on the other side of the Ganaraska river, welcomes visitors. It is a moving experience to listen to the rare old pipe organ with its recently added festival trumpet.

The original pews in the new church were sectioned pews for which rent was charged — fifteen dollars per annum for a large section and twelve dollars per annum for a small section. A number of free pews were provided at the back of the church for those in poor circumstances. Pew rental is a practice that ceased many years ago.

The original chandeliers were gas fueled. These fixtures were restored in 1987, the Edwardian shades adding greatly to the old-fashioned appearance of the church.

Most of the stained-glass windows were made in England and are typical Victorian memorials to families and individuals prominent in the founding of St. John's. The three large east windows together with the rose windows are a memorial to Jonathan Shortt, the Parish Rector for thirty-one years who died before the building was completed.

The window over the main entrance deserves special mention. It is a memorial to John Tucker Williams, a retired officer of the Royal Navy, a veteran of the War of 1812, and the first Mayor of Port Hope. The Welsh inscription at the base is roughly translated as: "Without God beside, nothing will come."

The magnificent old organ was originally a three manual "Traker" with mechanical action and considered quite rare. The pipework dates back to 1870, the console to 1896. Restoration and extensive repairs were done in 1978 and, in 1987, a festival trumpet was added to the organ.

The original bricks, which had been made of a soft local clay, began to deteriorate after one hundred and seventeen years. As a result of this, the bells of the carillon could not be rung for fear that the vibration would further damage the tower. An appeal was launched. Through the generosity, hard work, and faith of the congregation, eighty-five hundred bricks were replaced in the church and parish hall and a stabilizing cable was placed in the tower. On Thanksgiving Sunday, September 29, 1985, the bells once more called the people to worship after many months of silence.

High on a hill in the picturesque town of Port Hope, the beautiful Church of St. John the Evangelist calls the people to worship, while across the river, the story of the small "Mother" church continues. That first edifice did not stay closed for long, four years to be exact. It was re-opened in 1873 and re-dedicated to St. Mark. More alterations were done in 1895 and restoration took place in 1962. On July 26, 1959, Her Majesty Queen Elizabeth II and Prince Philip, accompanied by Governor General Vincent Massey, attended morning worship there.

Still in regular use, the quaint little white church offers the same message as St. John's across the river, "Come ye apart."

St. Mark's Church, Port Hope, a quaint old white clapboard building was first called St. John the Evangelist.

ST. LUKE'S CHURCH

ANGLICAN ❧ BURLINGTON

T he story of St. Luke's began in 1834 on a bustling street corner in the village of Wellington Square. A three thousand, four hundred and fifty acre parcel of land had been given to Joseph Brant in 1798 by the Crown in recognition of his loyal service throughout the French and Pontiac Wars and the American Revolution. Most of his people settled along the Grand River but Brant preferred the village of Wellington Square now known as Burlington. He built a fine home overlooking the lake and settled there with his third wife.

Joseph Brant was a responsible Chief who continuously endeavoured to help his people and further their interests. He is reported to have translated the Prayer Book and the gospel of St. Mark into Mohawk for his people. He planned for part of his land to be used for church purposes but he died suddenly before anything was done about it. This had to wait for his youngest child, Elizabeth.

That young lady, who preferred European dress over her native costume, married her cousin, William Johnson Kerr, the son of a Niagara Doctor. By 1834, when the people wanted an Anglican Church, it was the Kerrs who donated the land and started a subscription list for funds. The church was built quickly thereafter and was ready for services by the fall of that same year.

As originally constructed, it was a square two-storey structure. There was no narthex; the front doors were set flush with the wall, flanked by tall slim windows and were capped by a smaller triangular window shaped like the top of a gothic arch. Six rectangular windows, three up and three down, lined each side of the build-

The pioneer graveyard beside St. Luke's Church in Burlington is the burial place of some of the descendants of the famed Indian Chief, Joseph Brant. Be sure to read the sign on the parking lot.

ing. The tall spire was topped by a two-tiered cupola. All the windows were plain glass and the interior walls were whitewashed. The high pulpit was reached by a winding staircase. From the sanctuary hung a stuffed dove, emblematic of the Holy Spirit, which looked down upon the congregation seated on hard "free" benches in the second floor galleries. Only the more affluent members could afford to sit in the box pews on the main floor.

Changes have taken place over the years. Additions and renovations have modernized the church and the spire which was lost to lightning has now been replaced. A flash from the defective lightning rod passed through the roof striking the reading desk door, flung it on to the Communion table, then disappeared through the wall. The second floor was eliminated and the roof lowered. The building has been well maintained.

The ministers of that era travelled considerable distances over horrible roads. In winter, families would start out for church by sleigh in intense cold and had to stop several times at the homes of other families to warm themselves. On one occasion, a family started for home after an evening service and all perished from exposure when they lost their way in a storm. The churches of today owe much to those early clergymen who persevered under such circumstances.

In later years, the fifth rector of St. Luke's, Rev. George W. Tebbs, developed quite a different form of mission, one entirely new to Canada. He arranged to have services broadcast from CKOC in Hamilton, beginning an association which lasted over eleven years. In 1931, this was extended to daily broadcasts and Mr. Tebbs was given the title, "Old Man Sunshine". His cheerful daily messages helped many listeners to weather the grim days of the Depression.

The pioneer graveyard beside the church is the burial place of some of the descendants of Chief Joseph Brant and the early settlers. The sign on the adjacent parking lot is in stark contrast to the ancient tombstones. It says, "Except thy vehicle be designated by St. Luke's, it shall not transgress herein. Private Parking By-Law 71-1983."

ST. MARK'S CHURCH

ANGLICAN ❧ NIAGARA-ON-THE-LAKE

The building of this beautiful old church was begun in 1804. Work proceeded rather slowly and it was not until August, 1809, that the first services were held there, with an assured revenue of three hundred pounds from the rental of the box pews.

St. Mark's was a substantial stone building, rectangular in shape, with galleries around three sides. Just as the congregation increased and progress was being made, disaster struck with the beginning of the War of 1812.

At that time, services were conducted by Rev. Robert Addison, the Missionary to Niagara, who had been there since 1792. He was also the Chaplain to the troops at Fort George. His parishioners included Lieutenant-Governor John Graves Simcoe and Mrs. Simcoe and Colonel John Butler. Major-General Isaac Brock was also a devout worshipper and contributor and it was Addison who conducted Brock's funeral after the battle of Queenston Heights.

When the Americans captured the town of Niagara on May 27, 1813, the church was requisitioned for the use of the army. It served as hospital, storehouse and kitchen. Army butchers used the low gravestone of Charles Morrison as a chopping block and the scars on it are still visible.

When the invading force retired to Fort Niagara on December 10 of that year, they burned the church along with the rest of the town. Only the stone walls were left standing. Fortunately, Rev. Addison's fifteen hundred book library, the oldest surviving library in Ontario today, escaped destruction because it was housed in his own home, a couple of miles outside town.

After peace returned, repairs to St. Mark's were begun. The building could be used only in summer until 1822; then it was finally consecrated in 1828.

There followed a period of prosperity and productiveness. The church's present outline was assumed in 1843 with the addition of the trancepts and sanctuary. The high pulpits were necessary so that those in the galleries might see and hear the rector without difficulty. At that time the beautiful chancel window of Belgian glass was installed, and the tablets bearing the Creed, The

St. Mark's Church, Niagara-on-the-Lake, takes you back to the War of 1812. The beautiful stained glass windows each have a story to tell.

Lord's Prayer and the Ten Commandments as well as the Bishop's Chair were brought from England.

Many other additions and improvements have been made over the years. The church tower received a chime of six bells in 1877, with three more added in 1917. In 1891, a chancel was formed at the front of the church to accomodate the choir and organ. This was moved in 1963 into the gallery at the back of the church to make room for a more spacious sanctuary. The pipe organ was enlarged and a graceful communion rail and new baptismal font were added.

Since then, considerable beautification of the sanctuary has been carried out. Needlepoint designed by the Royal School of Needlework shows the products of the Niagara Peninsula. It was donated by the late Mrs. Kathleen Drope and the needlework was done by ladies of the parish. Mrs. Drope's project extended to provide kneelers for the communion rail which was dedicated in 1978. The cover of the sound box is of hand-woven material made by another member of the parish.

The magnificent windows of St. Mark's Church were installed between the years 1843 and 1964 and are excellent examples of the artistic taste of those years. Enter by the main door and, turning left, go around in a clockwise direction:

1. *Randall Memorial Window*

Mr. Randall was a pharmacist at the Niagara Apothecary, so it was fitting that the main panel should show St. Luke who was a physician. Luke carries in his right hand the caduceus, which is emblematic of the healing professions.

2. *Garrett Memorial Window*

A finely executed design shows Christ preaching from a boat on the sea of Galilee, with ships and town in the background and birds overhead. The base panel at the left shows the Bread of Life symbolized by a sheaf of grain and at the right the Light of the World symbolized by a lamp.

3. *Anderson Memorial Window*

Dr. Anderson, one-time mayor of Niagara, was also the town's beloved physician for more than forty years. His window shows Christ blessing the children, surely appropriate for one who must have brought many of the town's citizens into the world.

4. *The Resurrection Window*

This window was installed in 1896. It has many unusual features and is one of the most beautiful stained-glass windows found anywhere. You are looking out from inside the Tomb on Easter morning with the angel pointing: "Behold the place where they laid Him (Mark 16:6). There are several layers of glass, giving a three-dimensional effect. The faces are inset under the robes as are also the hair, arms and feet. The use of mother-of-pearl glass for the angel's wings and robes makes him glow even though other windows are darkened by the lack of light. Against the central cross, on distant Calvary, there is a ladder with seven rungs. Seven equals perfection: Christ made the perfect sacrifice. The gibbous moon of early dawn enforces the message of a new day for mankind.

5. *Alma Memorial Window*

Mary and Joseph present Christ in the Temple with an offering of two young pigeons. Simeon stands ready with the circumcision basin against a background of the lake and the desert hills beyond, dotted with olive trees.

6. This *plain* glass window is of the style which was that of all the windows before the installation of stained glass. Being in the north vestibule, facing Lake Ontario, its only adornment is the naval cable and anchor.

7. *The East Window*

This is the oldest window in St. Mark's (1843). Made of Belgian glass, it depicts for the most part ecclesiastical symbols: mitre, key and staff, Bible, Cross and Dove; an equilateral triangle (the Trinity) comprised of the Greek letters for Christ and Jesus and a Trefoil.

8, 9, 10, and 11 — show Jesus at various stages of his life.

12. *The Rodger Memorial Window*

This was the last to be installed in 1964 and is of more modern design. In direct sunlight it is a blaze of colour, the rich colour of red and blue giving it a jewel-like quality.

Truly, St. Mark's Church is an inspiration to all who worship there as well as to the casual visitor.

THE CHAPEL OF
THE MOHAWKS

ANGLICAN ❧ BRANTFORD

I n 1784 the Six Nation Indians, who had allied themselves with
the Crown during the American Revolution, were granted a
large tract of land along the Grand River. Some four hundred and
fifty Mohawks formed a settlement in one part of it that became
known as "Mohawk Village". It comprised about twenty-four
houses, a chapel, a school and a Council House. In 1841, the establishment of what is now known as the Six Nations Reserve was provided by the Crown and the inhabitants of the village moved there
soon afterwards.

St. Paul's, the first Anglican Protestant church in Ontario,
was built in 1785 and is said to be the oldest surviving church of any
denomination in Ontario. The late Rev. Canon W.J. Zimmerman,
M.A., B.C. recorded much of the history of this church in his two
publications "Chapel Notes" and "The Story of the Windows".

The timbers were cut at Paris and floated down the Grand
River. The lumber used for the original siding was sawn by hand
and even the nails were hand made. The original floor remains to
this day. The front entrance was facing the Grand River as that was
the main traffic route of the era. It has since been moved to the
other end of the church facing the road.

St. Paul's Chapel of the Mohawks, Brantford, in its serene setting on the Grand River, brings to life the historical events of the late 1700's through its exceptional windows.

The Bell, cast in London, England, in 1786, was the first bell to ring in Upper Canada. At one time, it was consigned as scrap destined for New York but public opinion refused to relinquish it. The bell was retained and is now placed in its present position beside the chapel.

The Coat of Arms, one of the finest in Canada, was presented by George III and was carved out of one piece of wood.

A famous Iroquois symbol called the Pine Tree of Peace was behind the Cross. The beadwork was done by the Caughnawaga Indians nearly two hundred years ago.

Over the Altar are the Apostles' Creed, the Ten Commandments and the Lord's prayer in the Mohawk language.

The red carpet in the centre aisle was used in 1939 by King George VI and Queen Elizabeth during their visit to Brantford. The gold carpet in the sanctuary was in Westminster Abbey during the crowning of Queen Elizabeth II.

Until 1970 when the Mohawk Institute closed, services were normally held at the chapel every Sunday during the school year and the Queen Anne Communion Service was used on the first Sunday of the month at the Holy Communion Service. It bears the inscription: "The gift of Her Majesty Anne, by the grace of God, of Great Britain, France and Ireland, and of Her Plantations in North America, Queen to Her Indian Chapel of the Mohawks".

The Queen Anne Bible has this reference on the front cover: "For Her Majesty's Church of the Mohawks, 1712".

In the late 1950's, the Lord Bishop of the Diocese of Huron and a local committee made the decision that memorial windows be placed in the chapel and that they should take the nature of recognition of the Six Nations Indians and their role in Canadian life. Each window depicts some focal point in Six Nations history and through these symbols one is challenged to further thought and reflection.

Window number one draws attention to the founding of the Five Nations, which later became the Six Nations. The Pine Tree of Peace is a sacred symbol to the Indian People. Its roots run in all directions revealing a note of universality. At the base of the tree there is a hole in the ground with an underground stream, the purpose of which was to banish forever that which contributed to the brutality of life. In some interpretations of the Pine Tree of Peace, the two deer around the trunk symbolize the messengers of good will. The five objects in the Hiawatha Belt symbolize the five nations while the Golden Eagle overhead emphasizes the need for constant vigilance.

Window number two depicts the visit to Queen Anne's Court, in 1710, by Indian sachems, when a request was made for a chapel and ministry in the Mohawk Valley, and the pledge of loyalty was made to the Crown. The wampum belt show six figures joined together in the centre by a church, indicating the association of the Indian People with the Christian Church.

When the Six Nations Indians sided with the British during the American Revolution, cost to the Indians was deep and personal. They lost their lands, their homes and, many of them, their lives. In window number three, we see Joseph Brant, the celebrated Indian Chief, about to lead his people across Lake Ontario. The burning bush symbolizes the fires of revolution which swept America. At the top of the window an arrow points upward with two red elongated objects on either side. The Indian has his own way of expressing the great truths of life, i.e. if you shoot an arrow into the sky in anger, sorrow, like great drops of blood, shall fall upon the earth.

The fourth window shows Joseph Brant receiving The Reverend John Stuart, the Society for the Propagation of the Gospel Minister, who had been with the Six Nations in the Mohawk Valley. He journeyed from there at Joseph Brant's request to dedicate the chapel. The handclasp shows the warm relationship between the Indian and non-Indian families as they dwelt in the Mohawk Valley. At the top of the window, the Masonic symbol indicates Joseph Brant's connection with the Masonic Order.

Window number five reminds us of the love of God and its missionary outreach to all men. It depicts the consecration of the chapel in 1830 by The Right Reverend Charles James Stewart, Anglican Bishop of Quebec. A pictorial reproduction of the first bell in Upper Canada is at the top of the window.

Queen Elizabeth II granted permission for the Royal Cypher to be placed in window number six which has been called the Queen's Window. An Indian catechist passes out portions of scripture from the steps of the sanctuary, the first translation of the Gospel of St. John by the British and Foreign Bible Society.

The importance of education in the life of the Six Nations people is stressed in the seventh window. It pays tribute to the work of the Mohawk Institute, a residential school for Indian boys and girls (1831-1970) built by the New England Company, and honours a former pupil and teacher, Miss Susan Hardy, who taught there 1886-1936.

Number eight shows the Ascended Lord against a background of the Cross, with a trillium at the top of the window representing the Father, Son, and Holy Ghost. A figure at the left is offering the good earth, our natural resources. The figure at the right offers wampum from the manufacturers, craftsmen and tradesmen. These things are a symbol of the hope that the Indian People will have a place in the land where the Confederation Fathers planned that He shall have dominion from sea to sea.

Portions of the Mohawk Chapel were destroyed by fire in 1975 and 1976. The beaded black velvet hanging (reredos) behind the Altar depicting the Pine Tree of Peace was burned, the red and gold carpets and the Ten Commandments were destroyed. The carpets and the plaque have been replaced and the chapel restored.

On October 1, 1984, The Queen and Prince Philip visited Brantford. On the banks of the Grand River, leaders of the Six Nations Reserve pledged their loyalty to the Crown as their forefathers had done two hundred years ago. "Our people sacrificed everything, including their land, for their faithful covenant with the British", Chief Wellington Staats, head of the Reserve of approximately ten thousand five hundred members, told the assembly of nearly six thousand.

Links to the past were not just in the stirring words of Chief Staats but in the humble white clapboard chapel, in the silver communion set sent by Queen Anne in 1710, a treasured leather-bound Bible bearing royal signatures, and the glowing stained glass window known as the Queen's Window

A plaque was unveiled by Her Majesty and the little white church was designated as a National Historic Site. Her Majesty's Chapel of the Mohawks is the only Indian Royal Chapel in the world and the only Royal Chapel outside of the British Isles.

Uncle Tom's Chapel

NON-DENOMINATIONAL ❧ DRESDEN

One of Ontario's most popular tourist and heritage attractions is Uncle Tom's Cabin Historic Site on the outskirts of the town of Dresden. The Site contains a Museum, Agricultural Building, Smoke House, Former Slave House, Josiah Henson's house, and the Church.

The property on which the Site stands is part of two hundred acres of land, purchased in approximately 1842 at a cost of four hundred dollars an acre, to establish a refuge for the many fugitives from slavery arriving from the United States via the Underground Railway.

One of the slaves, Josiah Henson, was born into slavery in 1789 in Maryland, U.S.A. He remained a slave for forty-one years until his escape into Canada with his wife and children who were also born into slavery. Through those years of cruelty and degradation Josiah never forgot the prayer his mother had taught him — The Lord's Prayer. When he was eighteen years old, he heard his first sermon and was so impressed that he determined to learn more about being a Christian so that he could tell others that Christ died for *all*, even *him*. Although he could neither read nor write, he availed himself of every opportunity to learn new words and phrases. He began to preach to his fellow slaves, then to mixed congregations and was finally accepted as a preacher in the Methodist Episcopal Church.

With his little family, Rev. Josiah Henson settled down and built a home, now known as Uncle Tom's Cabin. He may have supplied many of the facts regarding slavery that were told in Harriet Beecher Stowe's famous novel "Uncle Tom's Cabin". Other buildings followed; a saw-mill, blacksmith's shop, carpenter's shop, and, of course, the church where Josiah preached for many years.

He became so well-known that he was sent back to the States to help others like himself and to solicit money to help build up the settlement. Several trips to England were also for the purpose of raising money. On one of those trips, Josiah Henson reached the enviable status of having shaken the hand of Queen Victoria. He was entertained by the nobility of England, a long way from the desperate life of a slave-boy.

Visit Uncle Tom's Chapel and the Museum in Dresden for a look back into the history of the underground railway.

In time, his little church was destroyed by fire. Only the original organ and pulpit were saved.

When the Historic Site Museum was formed during the late 1960's, a search was conducted by the Museum Committee to find another church which would closely resemble the one in which Rev. Henson preached his famous sermons. When they discovered that the old Windfall Orange Hall, situated near the town of Wheatley, was for sale, an investigation was made. The building (circa 1850) was the right size and age, indicated by the weathered siding, square cut nails and other architectural features. It had begun as a Presbyterian Church, then became an Anglican Church, and was finally sold to the L.O.L. 262 in 1903. The hall was moved to its present location where its weathered appearance and simple design blend in with the other buildings on the property and it appears as though is has always been there.

Uncle Tom's Chapel, as it is now called, has been well preserved. Thousands of visitors from North America and Europe step over the threshold, glance at the rough floor boards and pews, and stand in awe. The original pulpit and organ have been restored to their rightful place. You whisper because you do not wish to disturb the tranquility of this simple place of worship that honours the memory of a great man, Canada's most famous black person who found freedom for himself, his family and hundreds of fugitives.

WOODLAND UNITED CHURCH

WOODLAND SPRINGS

L ocated a few miles east of Mount Forest, north of Highway 89 on Woodland Springs Road, stands the quaint old Woodland United Church.

Its origin dates back to the fall of 1857 when a number of settlers decided to organize a congregation. It was the decision of those people that their church should be a Union Church because, at that time, many denominations were represented in the surrounding area. The Crown Deed, in fact, provided that "This church shall never be exclusively owned by any particular denomination of the Christian faith". From the first, however, Woodland Church was linked with St. Andrew's Presbyterian Church, Mount Forest, because the services were conducted for so long by a Presbyterian minister who considered Woodland to be an "Out Station". Such harmony prevailed that no one ever thought of the words in the original Crown Deed.

The first Woodland Church was a simple log building surrounded by a graveyard. It was in use until 1880 when the present brick church was built on an adjoining farm. Long after the new church was built, the little log chapel remained as a historic landmark in the corner of the cemetery. It was a crude building by today's standards, but it was in keeping with the times and served as a meeting place for twenty years. Then, in 1922, it was demolished and removed by a man named J. A. Ferguson who paid the sum of twenty-eight dollars for it.

The cemetery, the burial place of many of the area's early pioneers, is still used and beautifully maintained. A highway now runs north and south between the cemetery and the church.

When Woodland United Church had its 100th Anniversary in 1980, it celebrated by placing a plaque on the Woodland Spring down the road, dedicating it to the memory of the pioneers of the area.

Woodland Church has some unique features. It has two front doors, one on each side of a large triple stained-glass window. Its open, double bell steeple is different from most steeples. It is neither round nor square, but oblong, with the wide side facing the front of the building, thus allowing the two bells to be side by side.

When one realizes that the wages for men's winter work were fifty cents a day, seventy-five cents a day in haying time and one dollar a day during harvest, one can guess that money was scarce. Records also show that gifts of money to build the church ranged from fifteen to ninety-nine dollars. The fact that the foundation stone was laid on June 7, 1880, and the church was completed, dedicated and opened for worship in November of the same year, brings home to us the sacrificial giving of money, time and talent by those pioneers of faith.

A debate over the question of Union was a lively one stretching back to 1875 when there was unification of all branches of the Presbyterian Church. Over the years there were at least three votes in connection with the question of Union, culminating in the one favouring joining the United Church of Canada. In 1930, Woodland was realigned with the Mount Forest United Church.

About a quarter mile east of the church, a natural spring flows from the side of the hill. On the occasion of Woodland Church's Centennial in 1980, a special dedication service was held at the newly constructed Woodland Springs Memorial. What a marvellous way to celebrate one hundred years of a church's service beside the outpouring of God's precious gift of pure water! A plaque on the wall behind the spring tells it all: "Dedicated to the memory of the pioneers of the area on the Centennial of Woodland United Church, 1880-1980."

Woodland United Church stands high on a hill, beckoning people for miles around to come and worship, while just down the road, water pours from the hill to bless and refresh all who stop by with cup or jug.

THE CHURCH OF
THE IMMACULATE
CONCEPTION

ROMAN CATHOLIC ❧ MANITOULIN ISLAND

Beautiful Manitoulin Island with its rugged scenery, placid lakes and quaint towns with fascinating Ojibwa names, has more than its share of old, historical churches.

In 1648, Father Poncet was put in charge of a newly-created mission, formed to serve the Algonkian-speaking Indians of Manitoulin Island. He was the first known European resident there and served until he was compelled to abandon the mission in 1650 following the defeat and dispersal of the Hurons by the Iroquois. Wikwemikong is the largest of the Jesuit missions remaining on the island. Still active, it stands among the ruins of the old lime-stone schools, convents and houses, a photographers' paradise, as historic as they are beautiful.

St. Paul's Anglican, the oldest church building in the whole of northern Ontario, was built in 1847. The little Church of St. Francis of Assisi came into being later. Holy Trinity Church at Little Current was built in 1886

The Marine Church at Kagawong has many unique features besides its age. This tiny, white, shingle-covered building, well-maintained, stands with its back door practically in the waters of the North channel of Georgian Bay. This, of course, was for the convenience of sailors who came by boat. A large iron ring, embedded in concrete, is the only one remaining as evidence of the anchoring of small boats on the shore. On the outside wall, above the porch, is a ship's wheel. The small louvered bell tower is surmounted by the Anglican cross. The one modern touch to this pretty little church is the electric tubing outlining the cross, thus making it visible at night to boaters approaching the town.

Of all the churches on Manitoulin Island, the Immaculate Conception Church on the West Bay Indian Reserve is, without a doubt, the most beautiful and unusual. The twelve-sided, tepee-like structure recaptures the ancient Indian tradition of "meeting fire-pits" where they learned about the Spirit.

Unlike almost all other buildings described in this book, the church is not old. It was blessed and opened on June 22, 1972. It replaces a very old church that was destroyed by a propane gas ex-

The Church of the Immaculate Conception, Manitoulin Island, built like a teepee and sunk into the ground, recaptures the ancient Indian tradition of "meeting fire pits" where they learned about the spirit.

71

plosion on February 27, 1971, at which time one life was lost. Only a few items survived the explosion, among them a damaged bell which can be seen on one side of the entrance and a statue of the Virgin Mary which can be seen on the other side.

The beautiful hand-carved front doors are a work of art. The exterior surface shows the sun with four great rays coming from it. This is an ancient native symbol for the Great Spirit, the four rays in four directions symbolizing His universal presence and power. The sun is also the symbol of Christ, the Light of the World, with the four rays outlining the Cross. The twelve minor rays represent the twelve Apostles taking Christ's message to the four corners of the world and to all nations in obedience to Christ's command. The floral designs are typical Ojibway-Odawa motifs indicating the close association of the Ojibway-Odawa people with the Creator.

The Marine Church at Kagawong, Manitoulin Island, stands with its back doors almost in the waters of the North Channel of Georgian Bay.

The carvings on the interior of the doors gather together the main totems of the Anishinabe people. Each bird or animal represents a native clan or extended family, gathered together into one family — the Church.

Upon entering the church, you will be struck by its unique beauty. Its shape reflects the Indian tepee, with light coming in only from the central opening at the top. The community is gathered around a council fire. The colour blue to the natives means spirituality, and it is found in the royal blue carpet throughout. The rising tiers of seats suggest a hillside where Jesus gathered His people around Him. The building itself is round and everywhere you will notice the circle, a favourite symbol of native people, indicating the circle of life from the Creator through birth, growth, maturity, old age and death, back to God following the path of souls. Native people feel a closeness to Mother Earth, and so the church is sunk into the earth and from there rises up to the Creator, thus linking Earth to Heaven.

High above the Altar is a Thunderbird representing the Messenger of the Great Spirit, the Guardian Spirit of the Anishinabe people. The Altar itself is made of local black cherry wood. It is four-sided and is supported at the corners by four evangelists holding an eagle, a lion, an ox and a cherub, symbolizing the carrying of the good news of Jesus to the four corners of the world.

The Baptismal font rises from the back of a turtle, for it is the place of re-birth of the native people. According to legend, the Anishinabe people were re-established after the flood through the Sky Woman on the back of a turtle. The font, along with other accessories, were hand-carved by a local craftsman. The colourful hangings were also made by native artists. The colours of the four directions are symbolic and can be seen represented in the church — white for healing and life; red for warmth, fertility and growth; yellow for knowledge and new light; blue for spirituality and the soul's journey within.

The Immaculate Conception Parish community is now entrusted to a team of pastoral ministers which includes a Native

73

Deacon, Native ministers, Sisters of St. Joseph and visiting Jesuit Priests.

Inside this beautiful place of worship, the hundreds of visitors who come every year cannot but feel a tremendous sense of peace and tranquility and a oneness with our brothers and sisters, the Native People of Canada.

Peace be with you – "Animigagawin".

THE CHURCH OF MARY

NON-DENOMINATIONAL

☙ ST. JOSEPH'S ISLAND

St. Joseph's Island, lying north and west of Manitoulin Island, is also steeped in the history of the First Nations People and the Jesuit Missionaries.

High on a hill on the south shore, overlooking Georgian Bay, stands the Church of Mary. Built in 1876, it was the first church on St. Joseph's Island. It is probable that the same missionaries who taught the Indians on Manitoulin came across by boat to hold services here.

The church is quite isolated on a gravel road, having few homes nearby. Even so, it is well-maintained. Its white clapboard and green trim are so clean and fresh-looking it can be seen for miles. The building is small and of unusual design, almost as though a giant wishbone were inverted over the front entrance. Shrubs grow on either side of the double door. Looking upward to another arch and cross, one's eyes are drawn even further up to a small steeple topped by an upside-down cone roof and another cross.

The large cemetery with its freshly cut grass marks the burial places of the island pioneers; many tombstones bear Indian names.

The Church of Mary, St. Joseph's Island, is, in the true sense of the word, a real example of an old time country church complete with a matching privy with a half-moon cutout in the door.

A privy at the far back corner of the churchyard is of the same white clapboard with green trim as the church. The half-moon cut-out on its door completes the picture of country convenience, or perhaps a better word would be inconvenience.

Close beside the front of the church facing the Bay is an unusual lighthouse. The very name brings to mind a round or square wooden structure with a windowed cupola and revolving light. Not so, beside the Church of Mary. This one seems strangely out of place. Twice the height of the church, the modern steel structure is surmounted by a light and a large striped marker such as those used to chart the routes through narrow channels. Perhaps there are still treacherous rocks on the south shore of the island. It is unfortunate that the Government or whoever put the lighthouse there did not see the way it detracts from the simplicity of the little country church. In any case, both the light and the church perched on the hill act as a beacon to boaters as well as to others who come by car or on foot.

Although the Church of Mary began as a Roman Catholic house of worship, it was restored in 1980 as a non-denominational church beckoning all worshippers from its vantage point overlooking the blue water of the bay.

THE MADILL CHURCH

WESLEYAN METHODIST ❧ HUNTSVILLE

T he area where the town of Huntsville now stands was once an untamed wilderness of dense forest, rushing streams and placid blue lakes. Deer and moose had nothing to fear for there were few inhabitants.

Surveyors arrived in 1862 to make way for the many settlers who were looking for a place to build homes. Then in 1870 the Muskoka road, a crude trail, was extended to the site of Huntsville. The land was surveyed again in 1871 and the people soon followed.

One of these settlers, John Madill, took up residence and immediately donated an acre of land for a church and burying ground. Neighbours gathered together to form a congregation and made plans. They cut trees, skinned and squared them and donated the logs along with their skills. And so, in 1872, the Madill Church was begun. It was completed in 1873 and is one of the few remaining examples of a pioneer square-timbered church.

The foundation on which the Madill Church stands is built of loose, flat rocks laid in such a way as to overlap each other. The church itself is about thirty-six feet long and approximately twenty-seven feet wide. The timbers are, as an average, about sixteen inches square, so you can imagine the size of the trees they were made from. They were dovetailed at the corners and chinked with gray plaster. From the eaves to the peak of the roof, rough boards were nailed in an upright position. The whole exterior is weatherbeaten with age. The three windows on each side of the building are of old wavy glass. There are twelve small panes in each, with the two top panes shaped into the Gothic style.

The inside of the church is furnished with plain, rough wooden pews and floor boards. Behind a tattered curtain and wooden railing, a simple wooden table and pulpit stand on a small platform. The tongue and groove siding on the inside walls is painted a dull ivory colour and was probably added in later years. Old coal-oil lamps and a woodburning stove complete the picture of pioneer worship.

The Madill Church, Huntsville, is one of the few remaining examples of a pioneer square-timbered church.

The large well-kept burying ground, which is still used, has a perimeter of giant, gnarled maple trees which tower above the weathered tombstones of the pioneers, many of which bear the name of Madill. Some of them have been placed there quite recently, telling us there are still descendants in the area.

Mr. Hunt, a pioneer citizen after whom the town of Huntsville was named, is buried there.

The first services in Madill Church were conducted by itinerant missionaries of the Wesleyan Methodist Church. Although no longer in regular use, an annual service is held by the United Church of Canada.

Tucked away off the beaten track and practically unknown except to the local inhabitants, Madill Church stands tall in its serene setting, a beautiful tribute to the pioneers who carved a town out of the bush.

ST. JAMES-
ON-THE-LINES

ANGLICAN ❧ PENETANGUISHENE

This garrison church, erected in 1836-1838 on the Penetanguishene Reserve was attended by military pensioners and civilians. Until the 1870's it was the only Protestant congregation in the vicinity. Building funds were obtained largely through the exertions of the local naval commandant, Captain John Moberly, R.N. The first rector, Rev. George Hallen, held that post for thirty-six years.

Situated on the lines of communication between the Naval and Military Establishments and Fort York (Yonge Street to Holland Landing and the old Penetanguishene Road), the church became known as St. James on-the-Lines.

The actual construction of St. James was done by the soldiers and officers of the Establishments. Its wide centre aisle where famous military regiments marched four abreast, is only one of its extraordinary features. The pews are of individual construction. Different men of the garrison were detailed to make the pews and they did that job each in his own way. There is therefore a variety in the styles of the back rests. The front pew-ends are a little more ornate, thus marking the Officers' pews.

The military style screen or wall behind the altar, with its fine panelling and carved work, was crafted by a relative of the first rector about the year 1870. The man was very ill and, anxious to finish the job, lived in the church until it was complete. He died a short time afterwards.

One side of the double memorial panel is to the memory of Lieut. Wm. Glascott who froze to death after being thrown from a cutter while returning from town. There are two conflicting views as to why the other side was left blank. Some say it was to have been

Every July, soldiers from the nearby military Establishments march down the aisle four abreast in a St. James-on-the-Lines Anniversary service whose pageantry and colour make it a community event.

in memory of Mr. Glascott's traveling companion who was expected to die of pneumonia. However, the man recovered, was posted elsewhere and never heard of again. The other view is that it was left blank as a warning to soldiers against the dire consequences of intemperance.

Ornamental hinges on the west doors were hand-wrought by an unknown artisan from the Military Establishments, Penetanguishene.

In 1981, the Ontario Heritage Foundation designated St. James as an official historic site. Subsequently, members of the church's congregation, equipped with government funds and over sixty thousand dollars in private donations, engaged a restoration architect and initiated a program to arrest serious deterioration of the structure. Restoration was completed in 1985.

Although St. James holds a great deal of historical interest and is set in a quiet old cemetery with the oldest stone dated 1831 and where many of the community's pioneers and military leaders are buried, it is very much alive and active today. Services are held every Sunday at 9:30 A.M. In July of each year soldiers from the Establishments march again four abreast down the aisle, in an anniversary service whose military pageantry and colour make it a community event.

CHRIST CHURCH

ANGLICAN ❧ BOBCAYGEON

C hrist Church, Anglican, owes its beginnings to one Thomas Need, an Oxford graduate and adherent to the Church of England. He came to this country in 1832, fell in love with the beautiful wild untamed area known as Bobcaygeon or, as the Indians of that day would pronounce it, Bob-ca-je-won-uk.

Thomas purchased three thousand acres and built a log cabin. Soon he had a mill in operation, then a general store and a post office.

Slowly but steadily other settlers from the British Isles came, encountered and endured the hardships of the wilderness. They did not neglect the worship of God and opened their homes for Divine Services. As time elapsed and the congregation grew, they continued to meet in school, halls or wherever they could find a suitable place.

Mr. Need returned to England in 1844 but he left three acres in reserve for the building of a church. It was many years before the deed was finally registered and many more before the quaint church of today was opened in 1871.

Christ Church was designed by John Belcher, Architect, and his work and plans were donated to the congregation. The work of

The attractive one hundred and twenty year old Christ Church, Bobcaygeon, has shingles that resemble the scales of a fish.

building the church was done by local labour and tradesmen under the leadership of Mossom Boyd (lumberman) who was Chairman of the Building Committee and first Warden of the church.

This lovely old house of worship stands on a foundation of hand-chipped limestone blocks. The outside walls are made of vertical siding (board and batten), painted white. The steep roof, covered with shingles resembling the scales of a fish, is topped by a slim louvered steeple. The unique structure of this one hundred and twenty year old edifice is very attractive. It has been well maintained, the credit fcr which must go to all who down through the years have given of their time, talents, energy and financial support.

There are two large stained-glass windows at each end of the building, while smaller stained-glass windows are placed along the sides. The main entrance is on one side of the building.

More than a hundred and fifty years after the first congregation met in each others' homes, generations of children's children are still meeting in this beautiful church begun by the pioneer families. As the twig is bent, so grows the tree.

St. Thomas Church

ANGLICAN ❧ SHANTY BAY

T he Church of St. Thomas in the picturesque village of
Shanty Bay is one of the oldest original church buildings in
the Province of Ontario. It is also one of the few remaining structures in Ontario built of "rammed earth". In fact, it is said to be the
only building of this size constructed by this method, on the North
American continent.

The method of construction utilized wet clay mixed with
chopped straw, compacted into forms and covered, when dry, with
plaster or siding for protection against weather.

Built in a plain somewhat Romanesque style, with walls three
feet thick, it is a monument to the ingenuity and skill of the workers. The church is set on a massive stone foundation. The outer
plaster coating of the walls must have been perfectly sealed to keep
dampness out and to have preserved the building so well.

Begun in 1838 and largely completed by 1841, the design of
St. Thomas Church was copied from a church in Ireland. Col. Edward O'Brien, leading member of Shanty Bay Settlement, donated
the site of the church and the clergyman's residence and directed
the construction. He and his wife, Mary Sophia, are buried in the
adjacent cemetery.

St. Thomas Church, Shanty Bay, a picture-perfect church in a charming village, was patterned after a church in Ireland. The richness of history beckons.

The timbers used were the choicest white pine, white ash and cedar, all hand-hewn with broad axes and the lumber cut with whip-saws and pit-saws. The joints were fastened with dovetails or wooden pins.

The bell tower is a massive structure of squared timbers and contains a bell purchased in 1862.

As one enters the low, rounded arch of the doorway and on through the very small vestibule, the same Norman architecture can be seen as its counterpart in Ireland. The original severe square pews are still in use.

The interior has some very interesting features. The Greek lettering on the wall behind the altar was designed by Amy Frances Raikes, a member of the family who originated the Raikes Diploma Systems for Sunday Schools which are still in use.

The ancient organ, built in England in 1805, has been in St. Thomas Church since 1892. It required a helper to pump a handle connected to the bellows while someone was playing. This was done until 1938 when the organ was completely rebuilt and electrified. At that time the original manual, pedals and pipes were incorporated into the present instrument.

A chalice dates back to 1805; the lectern Bible used to this day, was presented by "The Society for Promoting Christian Knowledge" in 1842. Also on display are the Regimental Colours of the Grey and Simcoe Foresters. Col. O'Brien commanded that regiment when it was engaged in helping to quell the Riel Rebellion in 1885.

The Colonel's second son, Lucius, is buried in the cemetery where a simple, rough-hewn stone cross bearing only the letters "L.O'B." mark his grave. Lucius was a famous painter of the 1880's. He was born in Shanty Bay, educated at Upper Canada College and became an architect and a civil engineer. But art was his first love. He was a self-taught painter, excelling in water colours. Queen Victoria commissioned him to do two views of Quebec. When the C.P.R. asked him to do a series of cross-Canada views, it provided him with his own railway car and introduced him to the Rocky Mountains, the theme of some of his finest paintings. He was an active member of the Ontario Society of Artists and later became the first president of the Royal Canadian Academy.

Any visitors to the lovely district of Shanty Bay and the charming old St. Thomas Church can understand the urge to become a painter.

ST. PAUL'S
PRESBYTERIAN
CHURCH

LEASKDALE

The congregation of St. Paul's Presbyterian Church in Leaskdale first met together in 1862, built their church and for many years shared their joys and sorrows with each other through good times and bad. They built the manse in 1885 and, as the congregation grew, so did the need for a larger place of worship. The present church was built in 1908.

Shortly thereafter a bachelor minister, Rev. Ewan Macdonald arrived to tend the flock. After one year of service, he asked for a three month's leave of absence — he was going to be married.

The ladies of the congregation descended upon the manse, cleaned and painted, but were unable to have everything ready when Rev. Macdonald and his bride Lucy Maud Montgomery, arrived back from a honeymoon in the British Isles. It was some three weeks before they were able to set up housekeeping in the manse.

At the time of their marriage, Ewan was forty; Lucy Maud was thirty-seven. It is recorded that she didn't share a romantic kind of love with him. She wanted companionship and children. They had three sons, Chester, Hugh and Stuart. Hugh lived only two days and is buried in the Foster Memorial Cemetery. Rev. Macdonald was a morose individual lost in a private darkness of his own and he resented the fact that his wife was a famous author. He was anything but a kindred spirit, blind to her emotional needs. She was Mrs. Ewan Macdonald, minister's wife and keeper of his household but the companionship she longed for was not to be hers.

To the congregation of St. Paul's, she was a person apart, lovely and rare, moving among them quietly, always interesting and interested. She approached her duties as a minister's wife with dignity and dedication but no one knew the turmoil that went on behind her ready smile. Those with whom she worked would have been astonished by the unorthodox opinions she kept to herself and they never realized the iron control that kept her at her post. Her loyalty to her husband, to her role as his wife and to her status as an author demanded that she keep herself above criticism. In doing so, she suffered private agonies.

Lucy Maud Montgomery's escape was in her writing. Eleven of her twenty-two books, including several Anne books, were written during her sojourn in the Leaskdale Manse. She went back to her beloved birthplace, Prince Edward Island, as often as possible,

From St. Paul's Presbyterian Church, Leaskdale, comes the delightful and often surprising story of the charming and talented author, Lucy Maud Montgomery.

there to refresh her mind and spirit and gather strength to cope with her life at St. Paul's.

There were successes, of course, besides the publishing of her books. In October, 1923, she was the first Canadian woman to be made a Fellow of the Royal Society of Arts of England. Then, in 1935, she was awarded the Order of the British Empire by King George V. She died in Toronto in 1942.

As for Rev. Ewan Macdonald, he was known in Leaskdale as the world's worst driver — even with horse and buggy. He didn't seem to know where the middle of the road or the ditch was and hit every pothole. On one occasion, in 1920, he collided with the Sunday School Superintendant from the Methodist Church, which did little to endear him to that denomination.

When he bought his first car in 1918, Lucy Maud became a back-seat driver. From her vantage point she could see trouble coming and prodded him in the back with her umbrella.

Because that lady kept her innermost feelings to herself and appeared happy and serene to the congregation, they saw nothing of her private turmoil nor her husband's increasing state of depression. He became so melancholy that he believed himself destined to hell. The people of his flock never knew of the despair for his state of mind that filled Lucy's heart for most of their years together.

After fifteen years of service at St. Paul's, the Macdonalds left Leaskdale to go to another charge in Norval, Ontario. While Lucy lived in the Leaskdale Manse, her magic personality touched the lives of all those who knew her.

In 1965, a Lucy Maud Montgomery Day was held in her honour at which time a plaque, erected by the Ontario Historic Sites Board, was unveiled by Kathy Macdonald, grandaughter of the author. It stands across from the church on the front lawn of the Manse where Lucy spent so much of her time writing.

Many well-loved ministers' wives have graced the manse since then but perhaps none were as well-known as Lucy. Today, St. Paul's Presbyterian Church continues to be a thriving, caring congregation in the little town of Leaskdale.

ST. PAUL'S ANGLICAN, THE QUAKER MEETING HOUSE, & THE THOMAS FOSTER MEMORIAL

UXBRIDGE

By 1834 this part of Upper Canada was thickly wooded and inhabited predominantly by the Chippewas. The village of Uxbridge consisted of a few log cabins, a grist mill and barn, blacksmith shop, frame tavern and driving shed, a small cooper's shop, one store, the sawmill and a schoolhouse.

As early as 1809 there were, however, many Quakers in the area. Their religious beliefs were strong, making their church, the Friends' Meeting House as it was called, the focal point of their existence. A plain white clapboard structure built on Quaker Hill, a few miles out in the country, still stands, well-preserved and open for an annual service one Sunday in June. The Meeting House and the nearby Quaker Pioneer burial ground are marked by an Ontario Historic Sites Plaque.

An Episcopalian missionary travelling along the corduroy road from Kingston to York, stopped when the route divided. One trail went to Port Perry. The man decided to take the other trail and arrived in Uxbridge where he conducted the first Anglican services in a nearby barn. The congregation grew large enough that a church became a necessity. Completed in 1851, St. Paul's Anglican was a frame structure with a belltower built at the front of the church, making a sheltered north side opening onto a path leading to the church. A second wider gate at the south side was provided for horses and carriages. This small church flourished until 1881 when much renovation and updating was needed. The decision was made to build the present St. Paul's Church.

It was another seven years before its completion but today it stands as a beautiful tribute to the architect and the many talents of some of the early settlers. The fine woodworking of the Vicars family is evident in the hammerbeam arches and quadrafoil designs. In fact, the church resembles many medieval parish churches.

Each of the unusual hand-painted glass windows is a masterpiece. A visitor from Great Britain was ecstatic when he saw them for the first time. Being an expert on such things, he declared that they were priceless examples of Victorian hand-painting and could even identify the pottery factory (Staffordshire/Royal Doulton/Chelsea, etc.) where the painters had learned their craft.

The Quaker Meeting House (c. 1809), an Ontario Historic Site, holds an annual service in June.

The exterior of St. Paul's also has some significant features. The quadrafoil design appears many times in the brickwork. The unusual double chimney, which is at the back of the building, appears like an inverted "Y" and is of special interest to people with a knowledge of architecture and archeology.

Both the Quaker Meeting House and St. Paul's Anglican Church are steeped in history but there is another building in the vicinity which deserves a place in this chapter. The Thomas Foster Memorial Temple, a totally unique and original structure, stands on a hill in rolling countryside, six kilometres north of the town of Uxbridge. The design of the Temple was inspired by the Taj Mahal, India's architectural masterpiece.

Locally, the Thomas Foster Memorial Temple, the design of which was inspired by India's Taj Mahal, is often called "Foster's Folly". It is the last resting place of a former Toronto Mayor.

St. Paul's Anglican Church stands as a beautiful tribute to the talents of the early settlers. This building is an architect's dream.

Thomas Foster was a political figure, first as a controller, then as a member of the Federal Government in Ottawa, and finally as Mayor of Toronto in 1925, 1926 and 1927. With the end of his political career, the idea came to him of a Memorial where his daughter Ruby, dead at the age of ten, and his wife who died in 1920, could be buried. This would also be his own last resting place.

The fundamental motif for the design was the pyramid, the perfect form of architecture. The masonry of Indiana limestone is enriched with carvings. The windows, the work of Yvonne Williams, a well-known Toronto artist, are of hand-painted, fired and leaded glass. Harmonious in colour and design, they flood the interior with soft colourful light.

The floors are of rich-coloured terazzo and marble mosaics wrought in symbolic designs. On entering the Temple, one crosses the River of Death on which float water lilies and lily pads. The Greek letters "Alpha and Omega" radiate from the central motif, the laurel wreath of victory over death.

There is much use of Italian marble, bronze, Devon stone, even gold. Arches, balustrades and columns make up the beautiful interior under an acoustical ceiling of azure blue. Circling the lower part of the dome, above the great arches, in gold lettering on a field of graded blue mosaic is the inscription, "Take this my body for it is done and I have gained a new life, glorious and eternal".

The beautiful Thomas Foster Memorial Temple is open to the public on the first and third Sunday afternoons from June to September.

St. John
the Evangelist

F lorence Nightingale was the daughter of a well-to-do land-owner in Derbyshire, England. Her cousin, John Smithurst, lived near her home on one of the estates called Lea Hurst. Growing up together and with much in common, they fell madly in love. Mr. and Mrs. Nightingale disapproved of this attachment and took Florence to the continent where they travelled for several years.

Florence's ambition since childhood was to become a nurse. As she travelled to various cities she learned all she could about nursing and hospital organization as it was then. When she finally returned to England, John was waiting and asked her to marry him. Influenced by her parents, she refused his proposal. Hurt and discouraged, he asked her what he was to do with his life without her. She replied, "I would like you to be a missionary to the Indians in North America."

In obedience to her request, John gave up his business and began training for the new work. In 1839 he set sail for Canada. At the end of a long ocean voyage and a difficult trek across the country, he arrived at the Red River Settlement, now the city of Winnipeg. There he became the first Canadian Church of England

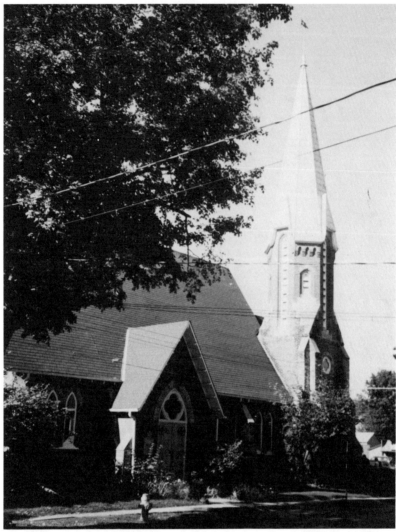

*The Florence Nightingale Window and the silver Communion Service seen in
St. John the Evangelist Church, Elora, are evidence of a poignant love story.*

Missionary to the Indians. He went first as Chaplain of the Hudson's Bay Company but soon obtained permission to minister exclusively to the local natives. For twelve years he worked tirelessly, suffering great hardships and privations, then returned to England to try once more for the hand of Florence Nightingale.

Disappointed and unrequited in his love, John returned to Canada in 1852, this time to St. John's Church in Elora, Ontario, where he became Rector. Certain by now that he would never have Florence as his wife, he threw himself wholeheartedly into the work. Under his guidance, the Parish progressed and flourished, later extending to Fergus.

While he pursued the career his beloved had chosen for him, he challenged her to do the same. If she could not have John, Florence would never marry at all. With that decision, she systematically pursued her own chosen profession.

When a call came from the Crimea in October, 1854, Florence accepted. Unable to lavish her love on one man, she could care tenderly for thousands. With her band of forty-two trained nurses, this Lady with the Lamp, as she became known, sacrificed her health in the Crimean War and was ever afterward an invalid.

When her lover learned of her unhappy state, his health, too, began to break. Their last lingering hope of a life together was gone. He retired to a secluded life on a bush farm where he lived quietly for ten years. When Reverend Smithurst's health failed utterly, he returned to St. John's Rectory where he was cared for by his successor. He died in 1867 at the age of fifty-nine and was buried in the Elora Cemetery.

Renunciation brought no unique opportunity to him but, in Florence's case, it made history. Their loss of happiness was the world's gain. All may sympathize with these two who highly resolved to give up the chance of happiness, to accept the cross of loneliness and take upon themselves a life of service. Their love story ranks among the great love stories of history.

The visible sign of their tender and abiding attachment is a beautiful Communion Set which is now in the Church of St. John the Evangelist in Elora. On the underside of one of the pieces, a Latin inscription is engraved: DONO DEBIT HOC MUNUSCULUM REVERENDO JOANNO SMITHURST AMICO DELICTISSIMO. Translated, it means: "Acting as agent for someone, Ebenezer Hall gave, as a gift, this set of Communion Silver to Reverend John Smithurst, a very dear friend, in grateful recognition of his many kindnesses. A.D. 1852." Although the name of the "someone" was not mentioned, there is no doubt that the giver was Florence Nightingale.

That silver communion set is on display in the church* and was used for over one hundred years in the sacrament of Communion. One of the beautiful stained-glass windows in the church depicts John Smithurst holding his Bible, another shows Florence Nightingale, The Lady With the Lamp.

---

* The two historic chalices were reported stolen just as this publication went to press.

THE CHURCH OF
OUR LADY

ROMAN CATHOLIC ❧ GUELPH

T he majestic Gothic Church of Our Lady Immaculate which
dominates the skyline of the Royal City of Guelph is one of the
most beautiful ecclesiastical edifices in the Western Hemisphere.

The hill on which it stands was given to the Catholic Church
by John Galt, when he established the new settlement of Guelph
on April 23, 1827.

Father Campion, the military chaplain at Niagara, celebrated
the first Mass in August of that year. Until 1831, Mass was celebrated
in the home of Mr. Lynch, the blacksmith, then in a schoolhouse
which was also used by the Methodists and Presbyterians. In 1835, a
small wooden church was constructed on the hill, the first painted
structure in the settlement. St. Patrick's, as it was called, served the
parishioners until 1844 when it was destroyed by fire.

The little wooden church was not replaced until 1846 when a
small stone church was dedicated by Father Thomas Gibney who
had been the first resident Pastor since 1837. Shortly after the
dedication, he was killed in a riding accident. The years following
that event were difficult ones for the parish. Those already settled
were poor and many more Irish immigrants arrived fleeing the po-
tato famine in their homeland, destitute and often ill.

A new era in the history of the parish began in 1852 when Father John Holzer, S.J. became Pastor in Guelph. For about eighty years, until 1932, the parish was under the care of the Jesuit Order. At that time it was felt that the Jesuits, whose calling was missionary and educational work, should move on and leave the responsibility of the parish to the diocesan priests. A plaque bear-

The magnificent Church of Our Lady in Guelph was built in the style of the world famous Cologne Cathedral in Germany.

ing the inscription, "In honour and loving memory of all the Jesuit Fathers and Brothers who were associated with the Church of Our Lady, Guelph", was placed on a pillar in the church.

Father Holzer was a great organizer. He began work on a large stone schoolhouse which later became a convent. He also built a rectory, then, in 1861, founded St. Joseph's Hospital. Construction of another was begun with the laying of the cornerstone in 1863 but the project was abandoned after a debt of twenty thousand dollars had been accumulated. Legend has it that Father Holzer was a friend of the Emperor Maximilian of Mexico who supplied the funds and that, when Maximilian was shot in 1867, the funds stopped and so did the building of the church. It is unlikely that this legend has a basis in fact as the problems of financing the church arose long before the death of Maximilian.

It wasn't until 1874 that plans for the present Church of Our Lady were begun under the direction of Father Hamel. He appointed Joseph Connolly, the man who designed many 19th century Ontario churches, as architect. The cornerstone was laid in 1877 and eleven years later the church was dedicated.

Unlike many of the magnificent old cathedrals built by kings and men of wealth, this one was built by the generosity, sacrifice and labour of the poor immigrant settlers. The Church of Our lady Immaculate has many similarities to the 13th century Cologne Cathedral, one of the most famous masterpieces of Gothic art in Germany. Therein lies its uniqueness. It takes the general form of a Latin Cross. It is composed of a spacious nave and chancel, boldly defined transepts of the closed order which carry the eye in unbroken view through the rich blue vaulted nave and gilded canopy to the Altar.

Over the years, improvements and renovations have been made. The Gothic towers were not added until 1926. Although now surrounded by shopping centres, stately homes and factories, amid the coming and going of modern day traffic, Our Lady still stands high on the hill, seen for miles in all its splendour. It is open every day of the year inviting all to enter and rest, regardless of race, colour or creed, rich or poor, sick or well.

ST. JOHN
THE EVANGELIST

ANGLICAN ❧ ROCKWOOD

A nother of Ontario's architectural gems is the Church of St. John the Evangelist in Rockwood. Built in 1884, it sits on the highest point of land in that village.

At the time of the building, the congregation was made up of millers, yeomen, sawyers, stone masons, stone cutters, farmers and their families. They gave freely of their essential and valuable talents. The land was donated by one of the first members, Squire Henry Strange, who owned a quarry from which came the exterior limestone blocks.

Times have not changed. Congregations have been restoring and maintaining this beautiful church for over one hundred years. On the inside, graceful arches are ornamented by sculptures, finely executed in plaster. As in most of the old churches, the beautiful stained-glass windows are a joy to behold.

Restoration over the years has been partially done by members of the congregation. The pine altar, credence table which holds the communion vessels and the small cupboard to the left of the altar were all made by local craftsmen. The women of the church stitched the needlepoint kneelers and cushions for the sanctuary.

The situation of the church on a rocky knoll posed some problems in landscaping but now, thanks to professional advisors, St. John's has a setting which enhances this lovely limestone building. The grounds were terraced and the steep bank to the northeast of the church was planted with periwinkle, junipers and cotoneasters almost entirely by the women of the congregation. Catalpa trees, a Hopa crab and other specimen trees were planted.

St. John the Evangelist church in Rockwood, built of local limestone, stands on the highest point in town overlooking the "village green".

And where in Ontario will you find a "village green"? Right here in Rockwood. Benches were installed on the spacious lawn at the bottom of the hill and the whole community invited to enjoy this little corner.

Gone is Joseph John Aldous, the vestry clerk who served in that capacity for fifty-three years. Gone also is the potbellied stove which brings back many humorous memories. The first settler in Rockwood became the Sexton whose job it was to tend the stove. In the middle of a (too long?) sermon he would stump up the aisle to poke the fire, making a great deal of noise, much to the annoyance of the Priest.

The village of Rockwood celebrates many special days in the year, some of them centered around St. John's. As Christmas nears, the Nativity scene appears on the village green and traditional carol singing takes place around it. The carollers are then warmed by a bonfire and cups of hot chocolate.

Mothering Sunday takes place during Lent. In a simple but very moving ceremony, children go to the altar to receive flowers which they then give to all the mothers in the congregation as a token of love and thanks. After the service, the traditional "simnel" cake, a rich fruit cake covered and decorated with almond paste, is served. The cake is a symbol of plenty.

Easter, as in all churches, is very special as is the Harvest Festival. At the latter, families take the responsibility for decorating a window. There are sheaves of wheat and a special braided loaf on the altar. Blessed and used at Communion, it is donated by Herb Saunders, a local baker. Mr. Saunders donates the bread in a spirit of ecumenical friendship as he is a Roman Catholic.

Since the church is now clearly visible from Highway No. 7, many passers-by stop to look at and admire St. John's. It remains a sanctuary in time of trouble, a joyful meeting place for festivals, a truly beautiful church built to the glory of God and preserved for future generations.

TRINITY CHURCH

ANGLICAN ❧ BOND HEAD

Missionaries travelling in the area of Bond Head were holding well-attended services in homes and barns as long ago as 1833. When the small St. John's church was finally built in Tecumseth Township in 1837, the Reverend F. L. Osler was installed as pastor. He was not happy with the living arrangements made for him. The rectory was a makeshift house in what was formerly a stable in Bond Head. At the end of one year, Rev. Osler stated that unless a proper residence could be provided he would have to leave the parish. The sum of three hundred and sixty-eight dollars was raised, an acre of land was donated and so began an arduous term of his ministry.

The licensed charge at that time extended over two hundred and forty miles of country but the outstations extended over two thousand square miles, taking in Coldwater, Medonte, Penetanguishene, Barrie, Shanty Bay, Caledon and intermediate places. His mode of transportation was, of course, horseback. Many times he requested help but was refused. Finally, an arrangement was made with the Bishop of Montreal to institute a college and six suitable young men came to train for the ministry. The Osler

Trinity Church, Bond Head, was the religious training ground for many prominent Canadians.

Theological College flourished for a few years and another church, Trinity Anglican, was built on the 7th Line.

In 1843 Mr. Osler left for England completely broken in health. More than one hundred and ten sleighs and wagons filled with parishioners accompanied him as far as Holland Landing as a token of love and respect.

His health improved enough to preach in London and Ireland where he contacted the House of Lords, the House of Commons and other influential people. With their help, he was able to return to his parish with a great deal of financial aid.

Rev. Osler picked up his work where he left off. He and his wife, Ellen, had four sons; each of whom made a great contribution to the development of Canada. The eldest Featherstone Osler became a lawyer, was appointed to the Appeal Court of Ontario, and declined an appointment to the Supreme Court of Canada offered him by Sir John A. Macdonald.

The second son Britton Bath Osler became a brilliant criminal lawyer and, in the 1890's, dominated the Canadian legal scene.

The third son Edmund Boyd Osler rose quickly in the realm of finance, was knighted in 1911 and remained a power in Canadian banking. He was also a member of the House of Commons for West Toronto for twenty-one years.

The most remarkable of the four sons was William the Doctor. He was a Professor of Medicine at John Hopkins University for fifteen years and then, in 1904, was appointed Professor at Oxford, England, a post he held until his death in 1919. He was created a Baronet a few months before Edmund was knighted.

Reverend and Mrs. F. L. Osler and their four sons, through their service to Canada and through Sir William to the world, have for all time put the district of Bond Head and Tecumseth on the map.

Another distinguished Anglican parishioner of the Parish of Tecumseth was the late Sir William Mulock, at one time Postmaster General of Canada. He was born in Bond Head in 1843 and died a centenarian in 1944.

In 1885 it was decided to move Trinity Church from the 7th Line of Tecumseth and re-erect it in Bond Head at its present location. On September 1 of that year, the taking apart of the church commenced and it was conveyed to Bond Head piece by piece in wagons. The church was re-assembled and opened for worship on its new site on December 20, 1885, just in time for the Christmas services.

The succession of ministers who followed Rev. Osler worked long and difficult hours to keep the church going. Rev. Canon Hearn, who served the parish for nearly forty-two years, was instrumental in helping the parish to survive in the spiralling economy of the twenties and the resultant financial crash which began the Depression years. He and his wife took over many other duties such as shovelling coal and tending the furnace. The stipend was often produce from the nearby farms. Their unselfish sacrifices preserved the parish through a difficult phase of its history.

Trinity Anglican Church, Bond Head, is justly proud of the many individuals from its parish who have made noteworthy contributions to our country.

THE TEMPLE
OF PEACE

SHARON

In the small village of Sharon, a half hour's drive north of Toronto, a remarkable edifice stands — a landmark in York Region for more than one hundred and fifty years.

It was built to conform to the vision of David Wilson, an immigrant farmer from New York State who settled on a two hundred acre farm in the village of Sharon in 1801. He joined the Society of Friends where he spent several years as their leader. However, he did not agree with some of the customs and beliefs of the Quakers and in 1812, with the support of several families, he formed The Children of Peace. For the next half century David Wilson served as leader of that sect and it was under his direction that the Sharon Temple was built.

The master builder, Ebenezer Doan, along with local farmers and craftsmen, began the work in 1825, each contributing according to his own particular skill. Seven years later, the Temple stood, its symbolic beauty an amazing achievement in the early 19th century wilderness of Upper Canada.

Sixty feet square at the base, the three storeys of this white frame building represent the Trinity. Its square base indicates that the Children of Peace meant to deal on the square with all people.

113

The doors on four sides are to let the people come in from every direction on equal footing. The equal numbers of windows on each side was to let the light of the gospel shine equally on all assembled. Twelve pillars symbolizing the apostles support the upper storeys. In the centre of the Temple stands the Ark which holds the Bible. Made of pine with butternut facings nailed in place, it is flanked by four more columns standing for Faith, Hope, Love and Charity, the foundation on which the Temple was built.

On the four roof-corners of each storey are white lanterns with gold tipped spires. Each September an illumination service was held when candles were lit in each lantern and in every window, one hundred and sixteen in all. Their brilliance in this backwoods village must have been a dramatic sight for miles around.

The beautiful Sharon Temple, now a museum open to the public, houses an 1819 barrel organ believed to be the first built in Upper Canada. Classical concerts are frequently held here.

Suspended from the lanterns on the top storey is a golden ball of peace, a symbol of world unity.

Music and worship were synonymous for David Wilson. A band and choir, which had been established in 1820, travelled throughout the countryside performing at political meetings and gatherings. Also in 1820, an organ builder named Richard Coates built a barrel organ for the Children of Peace. It is believed to be the first built in Upper Canada. Today it has been restored and is operated in the Temple for visitors. Two banners symbolizing Peace, carried during processions, were painted by the same man, Richard Coates, and are now on display.

The Temple was used only fifteen times a year for special religious and musical services while regular services were held in a nearby Meeting House which no longer stands.

David Wilson died in 1866 and was buried in the Sharon Burying Ground. With his death, the sect gradually declined. The last meeting was held in 1889. The Temple was neglected until 1917 when the York Pioneer and Historical Society bought it and began restoration.

The tradition of music begun so many years ago is being carried on at Sharon with classical concerts held in the acoustically superb Temple. A very successful festival began in 1981 to celebrate the Temple's one hundred and fiftieth anniversary and will likely be repeated in future years. Thus, the influence of the "Children of Peace" is still being felt by all those who visit this beautiful place.

THE FISHERVILLE CHURCH

EARLY PRESBYTERIAN ❧ BLACK CREEK
PIONEER VILLAGE, TORONTO

his quaint little church was built at the corner of Steeles Avenue and Dufferin Street in 1856, on property that originally belonged to Jacob Fisher, after whom the village of Fisherville was named. In the beginning it was a Presbyterian Church with an active membership of twenty-five. After the Union of some of the Presbyterian, Methodist and Congregation Churches, it became Fisherville United Church.

The church is a fine example of Greek Revival architecture. The stucco exterior is in keeping with the style of the building and provides an unbroken background to highlight the wood trim.

Stucco was an effective and visually pleasing exterior finish and was highly fashionable at that time. It was able to repel water yet, at the same time, to breathe allowing interior moisture to escape. The process involved covering the walls with a coat of plaster-like material made up of lime, sand and water, with the addition of animal hair and stones. Three coats of this were put over a split lath foundation wall. The first was a scratch coat, the second a brown coat, then the finish coat. The object of covering the outside walls was to imitate stones and some finishes were tooled to resemble cut stone.

Over the years, the stucco began to deteriorate. It was restored to its original condition and appearance and moved to its present location in Black Creek Pioneer Village.

The interior is simply furnished with a high pulpit and box pews, typical of early Ontario Presbyterian churches. There were no musical instruments used in those days and none are used to this date. Heat was provided by a wood stove neatly installed through the lobby wall, seen as you enter the front door. Long stove pipes carry the heat through the main room.

The gray painted walls and furnishings are rather sombre as are the box pews with doors, but that was the way things were in the 1850's.

Lighting, when necessary, comes from two chandeliers which hold six candles each but the sixteen candle sconces around the walls don't add much to the lighting. There are two windows in the vestry behind the pulpit with twenty-four panes each. There are

The Fisherville Church is right at home in the setting of Black Creek Pioneer Village, one of Ontario's major tourist attractions.

three windows on each side of the church and one at each side of the front door, each window containing forty panes of glass. There is also glass over the front door. On a sunny day, there would be no need for candle light.

Services are held from time to time by ministers of various denominations. For many years, a special service was broadcast from the church on Christmas Day by the staff of Radio Station CFRB. The church pulpit is adorned with boughs of greenery during the holiday season when visitors will hear the strains of appropriate carols piped in from the back of the church. During the year, the church may be booked for evening weddings.

It seems fitting that Fisherville Church is in Black Creek — a pioneer church in a pioneer village, reminding us how important a religious faith was to our forefathers.

ST. JOHN
THE BAPTIST

ANGLICAN ❧ OAK RIDGES

This lovely old church was built on the site of the Puisaye Settlement.

General Josephy Genevieve Count de Puisaye, a high-ranking officer of Louis XVI's army, settled in the area now known as Oak Ridges in 1789. He brought with him a group of fifteen exiled aristocratic French Royalists and their following of forty-one Frenchmen. Together they formed a military station.

These settlers were the first to come "en masse" up Yonge Street. They were refugees who had lost their land during the French Revolution. Their townsite ran north for eleven lots on either side of Yonge Street and was known as the Puisaye Settlement.

Upper Canada's first Lieutenant-Governor, John Graves Simcoe, wanted the settlement to provide a military safeguard for his young capital, York, in the event of an attack from the north.

Captain William Graham, Justice of the Peace in the Township of Whitechurch, wrote to de Puisaye and complained about the condition of Yonge Street south to the town of York. He said there had been grievous complaints that the road was closed up, allowing them to go only a mile or two with their teams. He begged de Puisaye to order his people to clear the logs and brush out of the roads that they had cut into the bush.

There is no doubt that the roads were in a very bad state but the French noblemen and their retainers were not properly equipped for the hard work of clearing land and road construction. Besides the lack of necessary tools for the job, they were physically unable to do the work. They tried hard until 1779 when they sold their land and moved elsewhere. De Puisaye then decided that Yonge Street was impossible for transportation. He abandoned his project and left the country for England.

Although the settlers had gone, it is assumed that some buildings were left behind and others soon found their way to the settlement. They came up the narrow twisting trail that was Yonge

When St. John the Baptist, Oak Ridges, was built, Yonge Street was a narrow twisting trail where treacherous holes, fallen logs, tree stumps and swampy spots were a constant danger to horses.

Street where treacherous holes, fallen logs, ugly tree stumps and swampy spots were a constant danger to horses. Hills were steep and streams unabridged. Broad tree branches were fastened to wagon wheels to prevent the wagons from rolling down steep slopes or sinking into the mud. Other travellers had to remove the wheels altogether and float their wagons across the Don River like boats.

The early 1800's saw many more settlers make their way to the Puisaye Settlement. They suffered years of privation and hardship but, in spite of it, they gathered a congregation together in 1846 and began construction of a church. In 1849 they began using it for regular worship. The first Bishop of Toronto, John the Strachan, consecrated the cemetery and Church in 1856 as the Church of St. John the Baptist. The graveyard contains the graves of many of those first settlers.

Since that time, the church has been added to and some parts restored, but the main body is still intact. It stands high on a hill on the east side of Yonge Street at the Jefferson Side Road, facing the constant flow of traffic up and down that wide and busy highway. The de Puisaye settlers are not forgotten and their story is told on the Historical Plaque beside the church.

The Anglican Church flag, a red cross on a white background with green maple leaves in each corner, flies proudly from its flagpole.

THE MARTYRS' SHRINE

ROMAN CATHOLIC ❧ MIDLAND

T he Martyrs' Shrine in Midland is an impressive church. In order to appreciate its significance, we must go back in time to the year 1639 when the Jesuit Fathers first brought Christianity to the Huron Indians. They laboured among the natives of the Georgian Bay area where they erected a small mission church at Ste. Marie, their headquarters.

Ten years later, when the Huron Indians and the Iroquois were at war, the mission was burned to the ground and the Jesuits fled in terror. A number of them were brutally murdered, among them Fathers Brébeuf and Lalemant.

Almost three centuries later, in 1926, a twin-spired church commemorating the eight martyred missionaries was built directly across from Ste. Marie. The Martyrs' Shrine, as it was named, stands majestically on a hill with a sweeping view of Georgian Bay. It is surrounded by beautifully landscaped grounds containing the Stations of the Cross and a miniature Lourdes Grotto.

The church is not only a shrine but it is a national tourist attraction which includes a theatre, guided tours, prayer gardens, souvenir shop, cafeteria, lookout and picnic areas. It is open from

Victoria Day weekend to mid-October when thousands of visitors from all over the world come in cars or buses.

It is a strenuous walk to the top of the hill behind the church but, once you've reached the lookout, you will be glad you made the effort. An historical plaque there calls the place "The Gateway to Huronia".

From this lookout may be seen the part of Georgian Bay which, during the first half of the 17th century, formed the western terminus of the 800 mile route which connected New France with the Huron Settlement of Ste. Marie. Heavily laden canoes ascended the Ottawa River, surmounted the treacherous rapids of the Mattawa and French Rivers, crossed Lake Nipissing and traversed the island-studded channels of Georgian Bay. Over these waters passed Récollet and Jesuit missionaries Etienne Brûlé, Samuel de Champlain and other heroic figures of early French Canada.

The story of the Martyrs' Shrine, Midland, goes back to 1639 when the Jesuit Fathers made a journey in faith to bring Christianity to the Huron Indians.

123

The blackrobes (as the Fathers were called) of 1639-49 who were stationed at Ste. Marie, surely must have stood on the same hill watching anxiously for the arrival of their brothers and the returning Huron canoe convoys.

Pope John Paul's visit to the Shrine on September 15, 1984, was called the "Journey in Faith". On his walk through the grounds, Pope John blessed the 60-foot tall wooden cross erected in his honour. The cross stands near the Papal Altar beside a beautiful piece of Quebec granite upon which is carved the date of the historic visit.

Also honouring the Pope's visit is a commissioned sculpture of Pope John Paul made from a 400-year-old white pine log from the Huronia area. In the beginning, the log was eleven feet high, four feet in diameter and weighed three thousand pounds. Ninety-five percent of the sculpturing was done by a chain saw, accented by small grinders. It was created by the combined talents of Thomas Penny of Orillia, assisted by Rex Hardin of Portland, Oregon, and Myles McDonald of Cumberland Beach.

This magnificent figure, as well as the church itself, stands as a fitting memorial to the brave Jesuit missionaries of the 17th century who also made a "Journey in Faith" to the Georgian Bay area and in doing so paid with their lives.

THE AFRICAN EPISCOPAL CHURCH

ORO STATION

B etween 1830 and 1850, many black families fled from slavery in the United States to freedom in Canada via the underground railway. Most of them settled in southern Ontario near Dresden. In 1831, nine black veterans of the War of 1812 accepted land grants in Oro Township, thus forming the only government-sponsored black settlement in Upper Canada. In time twenty-four families, one hundred settlers in all, came north and settled on the concession running north of Shanty Bay known as Wilberforce Street.

In 1838, Rev. Ari Raymond was sent from Boston to minister to the black settlement. For the first few years, blacks and whites worshipped together in his home which was north of the Barrie road on the west side of the Third Line of Oro Township. Rev. Raymond organized the people into a congregation and a one-acre plot of land was purchased in 1848 from Noah Morris, a black, for one pound. Part of the property was for a burying ground and, in 1849, the African Episcopal Church was built on the remaining portion.

The small rectangular building, about twenty-four by thirty-six feet, was constructed of local logs, left rounded on the outside.

Inside, however, the logs were squared and white-washed. Some time later, tongue and groove wainscotting three feet in height was added. There were only nine small pews made of ten or twelve inch boards. The rough wooden floor of six inch boards was unpainted. A small wooden fence separated the raised pulpit from the pews.

Services could not have been held after dark as there appears to have been no lighting in the little church. It must have been used in winter though, because a chimney hole high on the wall behind the pulpit indicates the long ago presence of a wood-burning stove. It is possible that the congregation brought lanterns with them on dull days. The one room must have been rather dull, having only four windows, two on each side, with twenty-four very small panes in each.

In spite of the size of the church, about forty families were served by the year 1870. The first minister after it was built was Rev. Richard Sorrick. He remained for two years and, as well as

This small building once known as the African Episcopal Church and marked with a Provincial Plaque, keeps alive the memory of some of the families of former slaves who dared to escape from bondage for a better life in Oro Township.

preaching, endeavoured to teach his flock what he knew of the basics of agriculture.

Mainly, the church was served by itinerant preachers one of whom was Rev. William Banyard who stayed for four years. Then Rev. R.H. Harris, an Anglican, was sent by the New England Missionary Society. Eventually, one of the settlers' own men, Elder Bush, led the services and kept the church alive.

The community flourished for awhile but the soil was poor and the climate harsh. The little band of settlers became discouraged. The work was hard and it was more and more difficult to make a living from the land. They drifted away to other parts of the province and the settlement was gradually abandoned.

It is not known for certain when the last service took place in the old African Episcopal Church, but it is thought three or four services each summer were held until the late 1930's. In 1949, the building was renovated by the Township of Oro when imitation log siding was put over the outside to protect the original aging logs. In 1980 the roof structure was reinforced and a new wood shingle roof installed. The interior remains much the same as its original state. Local records indicate that the last memorial service was held in 1979.

In 1981, vandals attempted to destroy the church by ramming it with two stolen trucks. Although much of the north, west and south walls were destroyed, the upper structure remained intact and was soon restored again.

In 1984, a service was planned to be held at the site when the provincial plaque to commemorate Wilberforce Street and the black settlement was to be dedicated. However,. a very heavy thunderstorm made it necessary to go to the Edgar Baptist Church for the service. The plaque was later erected on the church property at the intersection of Line One and the Shanty Bay Road.

Today, the little old church on its lonely corner in Oro Township, serves to remind visitors of those families of former slaves who dared to escape from bondage for a better life in Ontario.

CHRIST CHURCH

ANGLICAN ❧ ILFRACOMBE

O ne of the many old churches hidden away in Ontario's cottage country is the beautiful Christ Church of Ilfracombe. Drive northwest about eleven miles from Huntsville on the narrow, twisting County Road 2 and you will see it perched high off the road.

Built of rough-cut local stone and surrounded on three sides by dense woods, it has a sort of musty look and feel about it, reminding one of some of England's old stone churches. The beautiful stained glass windows are easy to see but you have to look carefully to find the door. It's around the back and quite small. The tall steeple topped with a bell and cross rises above the trees.

The church was built in 1886 and first opened for services in 1887, but it was not until ten years later, in 1897, that the first marriage ceremony took place there. On September 1, John Lillie and Lucy Ann Shaw were joined in holy matrimony.

Very little is known about John and Lucy. They were probably the son and daughter of local residents although the area was sparsely settled at the time and the town of Huntsville would not have been very big either. The newlyweds must have moved to

The parents of world renowned comedienne, Beatrice Lillie, were married in the old English style Ilfracombe Anglican Church.

Toronto shortly after their marriage because it was there that their famous daughter, Beatrice, was born the following year.

The Lillies were a musical family. When a second daughter, Muriel, was a few years old, she began to study the piano. Bea, as Beatrice was later called, followed in her mother's footsteps and became a singer, beginning her career in a church choir. No one seems to know what happened to John but, in 1914, the two girls and their mother went to England where they became known as the Lillie Trio. They enjoyed a long, eventful and successful career on world stages.

During that period, Beatrice discovered and developed her natural talent for comedy and, when she auditioned in England for a part in a revue, her particular skill at making people laugh resulted in a contract.

Beatrice Lillie returned to Ontario during World War I when she performed at a concert in the Officers' Mess of a Battalion from Huntsville. It is quite probable that she performed for the troops in other places as well.

Back in England in 1919, she became engaged to Robert Peel, great-grandson of Sir Robert Peel, a former British Prime Minister who created the London Police Force, members of which were called "Bobbies" in his honour. When her father-in-law died and her husband succeeded to his title, Beatrice became Lady Peel.

Her marriage proved an unhappy one for Beatrice and she was obliged to continue her career for financial reasons. When her husband died in 1934, she was left with a pile of debts and a 13-year-old son to raise. Her son, also named Robert, was killed during World War II in a Japanese air attack on his ship in the Indian Ocean.

Undaunted, Beatrice returned full time to the stage and starred in several successful shows in New York and London. In 1960, she brought her show to Toronto's O'Keefe Centre where her special brand of comedy and song were given a standing ovation.

While in London, the gallant lady of comedy became a favourite of Britain's Royal family. His Highness The Duke of

Edinburgh on March 14, 1989, unveiled a plaque in Toronto in memory of Beatrice Lillie. It was placed at an Edwardian building which had been the Carnegie public library when Beatrice was a young student living nearby.*

It used to be said that Bea was baptised at Christ Church Ilfracombe. Perhaps she was, but the present rector of the Huntsville Anglican parish of which Ilfracombe forms a part, says there is no record of this. Even so, the very fact that the parents of such a famous lady were married there, gives the people of Christ Church and Ilfracombe a sense of belonging to Beatrice Lillie. She was their girl.

When Beatrice died in January, 1989, at the age of ninety-four, at Henley-on-Thames in England, her death was written up in the local papers of the Huntsville district. Her obituary stated that Noel Coward once called Beatrice Lillie, Lady Robert Peel, the funniest woman in the world. Christ Church, Ilfracombe, may well be proud.

* The plaque is found at 1115 Queen St. West, in a City of Toronto public health building erected in 1908 and known as the Beatrice Lillie Building.

AN OLD ORDER MENNONITE MEETING HOUSE

WATERLOO

T he Mennonite Church came into being in Zurich, Switzer-
land, in 1525, at which time its followers were known as
Anabaptists, or Swiss Brethren. The name Mennonite was not used
until twenty-five years later. A small group of believers broke away
from the established church and, by doing just that, were cruelly
persecuted for many years.

In spite of such horrendous treatment their numbers grew
and spread through western Europe. After one hundred and fifty
years of persecution, many of them crossed the ocean and settled
in Pennsylvania in the Quaker colony of William Penn. They pros-
pered and finally spread even farther afield.

Of those who came to Canada, many made their homes in the
Kitchener-Waterloo area. In his book "Separate and Peculiar",
Isaac Horst, a Mennonite from Mount Forest, Ontario, describes
the way of life of his people as simple, the main idea being to keep
separated from the modern world as much as possible.

In keeping with their beliefs, they built their churches, or
"meeting houses", plain and simple. Some of the more recently
built houses are built of brick but the Old Order buildings such as

the one pictured a few miles west of Elmira, are long, low, white clapboard structures about forty by sixty feet.

Next to the church lies the cemetery with its rows of plain white tombstones, some of the names almost obliterated by time and weather. On all sides of the yard are rows of posts, generally unpainted, with heavy chains strung between them. On Sundays, especially when the weather is fine, there may be as many as two hundred horses and buggies, depending on the size of the meeting house, tied to the chains.

The Old Order meeting houses were all built in the same manner. When approached from the road, the women and children enter by the door in the gable end to the left to leave their bonnets and shawls. The boys enter the door which faces the road and sit on the upper benches to the right of the door. The benches

One of the Meeting Houses in the Kitchener-Waterloo area where the "old order" is practiced. Their structured life style represents for many a step back in time and sometimes is referred to as "separate and peculiar".

on the left are taboo as they are occupied by the girls. The door by which the men enter is in the centre of the gable end to the right of the door facing the road. The young people and the newly married have their own special section as do the older men and older women. The "Diener" which means servants, as preachers and deacons are called, always face the road. Wooden hat racks are suspended from the ceiling over the men's and boys' sections. Unless there is a specific reason to do otherwise, all services are conducted in German and are quite long.

If it happens to be Communion Sunday, services often last four hours. After the dispensation of the bread and wine, the people remain for the washing of each other's feet. Needless to say, this takes a considerable length of time.

The inside of the meeting house is as plain as the outside. The plastered walls are white but none of the woodwork is painted. Warmth in winter is supplied by heaters placed in the centre aisle. There are no curtains or pictures and no musical instruments such as piano or organ.

The Mennonites operate their own schools, taught by their own teachers. Their inherent traits of economy and industry prevent them from buying ready-made food and clothing, as much as is possible. It is the accepted practice to butcher and process their own meats. Many of the specialized trades of bygone days are practiced by the Mennonites, such as blacksmith shops, carriage makers and foundries for casting brass buckles for the saddlery trade. The men are skilled and industrious workers, most of them farmers. The women are excellent cooks and homemakers.

In every aspect of their lives, the concept of "plain and simple" is carried out, but the plain and simple meeting house is the focal point of their existence. As well as worship, other important decisions affecting the life of the community are made there. In today's society, the absence of divorce, juvenile delinquency, lawlessness, crime and violence, which is what the Mennonite Church and its way of life was founded upon, surely is a heritage worth preserving.

HIAWATHA UNITED CHURCH

RICE LAKE

When travelling Rice Lake by boat you will see on the north shore, a little south of the old railway bed, a beautiful white church standing like a beacon against the sky.

The church gets its name from the Hiawatha Indian Reserve, which has a history dating back to 1823. It began as a Wesleyan Methodist Mission which consisted of a school for training its ministers, the church, and a manse. Those original buildings were replaced in 1870 by the present edifice which has a tall bell tower and impressive spire.

The church can be seen from the village of Harwood, directly opposite on the south shore of Rice Lake. In 1854, the Cobourg and Peterborough Railway arrived in Harwood en route to Peterborough with passengers, lumber and goods, and later ore from the Marmora Iron Foundry. A crib bridge was built across Rice Lake but proved to be so poorly engineered and constructed that it was closed in 1862. The railway bed mentioned above is all that is left of that means of transportation.

After the bridge closed, when the lake froze over in winter, the minister and possibly members of Hiawatha Church were taken across the ice by horse and cutter to worship on the hill. The

Hiawatha United Church, Rice Lake, is situated on the Hiawatha Indian Reserve, home of the First Nation Mississagas.

lake is shallow and only three miles across at the widest part and, at one time, a row of trees was planted in the water so, in winter, people could find their way across the ice with butter and cream from the dairy in Harwood.

As early as 1828, Peter Jones, an Indian Missionary, visited the Mission and was appalled at the poverty of the native people. Even so, they shared willingly what they had. Mr. Jones was invited to stay for a meal with one family who had nothing to eat but flour mixed with fish spawn and baked as pancakes. The Indian people were very strict on the Reserve at that time. There was no drinking or crime and the Temperance Movement was very strong among them.

Peter Jones ministered to Hiawatha for some time and became famous as the inventor of the Cree "Syllabic" characters for Cree writing.

In 1980, the church was raised and a basement put underneath. A door leading down from outside the building gives access to other groups who use it for social get-to-gathers and meetings. Restoration of the interior has been done and outside work, including a paint job, is in the planning as future finances permit.

Still stored inside the church are the old long-handled birch bark collection boxes which have been replaced by hexagonally shaped plates. These two new plates are of birch bark bound together with sweet grass. They are decorated with maple leaves fashioned from dyed porcupine quills.

In 1990 the Hiawatha Church celebrated one hundred and twenty years of service. Now known as The Hiawatha United Church, it is easily accessible by road. A minister from the nearby town of Keene holds services each Sunday evening, summer, winter, spring and fall. This in itself, is quite an accomplishment for such an out-of-the-way place and is indeed a credit to the people of the Hiawatha Indian Reserve, home of the First Nation Mississagas.

METROPOLITAN UNITED CHURCH

TORONTO

In 1818 when the town of York, as Toronto was then called, had a population of under eleven hundred, a small group of Methodists recognized the need for a chapel. The Reverend Henry Ryan mortgaged his farm near Beamsville to provide the money for the purchase of a site on King Street between Bay and Yonge Streets, and a clapboard building thirty by forty feet was erected.

By 1831, when the city's population had reached seven thousand and the membership of the little chapel was two hundred and sixty-four, the need for a larger church became a priority. A building site was acquired on the south side of Adelaide Street and a new two-storied church was opened in 1833.

Thirty-five years later, when the Wesleyan Methodists of Toronto decided to purchase, for twenty-six thousand dollars, a piece of land bordered by Bond, Queen and Church Streets and known as McGill Square, the Adelaide Street church was closed and later demolished. The dedicated members from the old Adelaide congregation were the nucleus from which the Metropolitan Wesleyan Methodist Church grew. The cornerstone was laid in August, 1870, by a former minister, The Reverend Egerton Ryerson, D.D., LL-D. The grand new church, dedicated in 1872,

Metropolitan United Church, Toronto, is steeped in the history of that city. Its magnificent windows and organ with nearly 8,000 pipes are just a few of its many tourist attractions.

became known as the "Cathedral of Methodism" and was acclaimed far and wide as a centre of fine preaching and beautiful music. In 1925 it became part of the United Church of Canada.

On January 30, 1928, a disastrous fire almost destroyed the church. In her book, FIRM FOUNDATIONS – A CHRONICLE OF TORONTO'S METROPOLITAN UNITED CHURCH AND HER METHODIST ORIGINS, 1795-1984, published in 1988, Judith St. John, a longtime member of Metropolitan, describes the fire. "Shortly after 4:00 A.M. an employee of St. Michael's Hospital across the street, noticed smoke coming from the church door facing the hospital. Firemen were on the scene within minutes but the fire spread quickly. Stained glass windows were smashed, slates fell from the blazing roof and the floor burned through and collapsed into the basement. Two hundred firemen from ten different stations fought the blaze, taking turns holding the twenty-six lines of hoses that poured water onto the inferno. It was so cold that the firemen's coats and hats became coated with ice.

Thirty-five policemen kept the area free of traffic. When the fire was finally extinguished, the tower, carillon, narthex and rear balcony were saved. The Sunday School and parsonage were unharmed. Unfortunately, the organ was completely destroyed, its pipes twisted into grotesque shapes. But the brick walls of the sanctuary stood firm."

Undaunted by such a tragedy, the congregation reconstructed the church. Today the magnificent stained glass windows are cherished Christian symbols. Miss St. John also describes the Communion table as the focal point of the chancel. The front face is a carving of the Last Supper, after the painting by Leonardo da Vinci. Carved from soft California oak, it is made from many pieces dovetailed together with the grain running in alternate directions to prevent warping.

The organ was built by the Casavant Freres of St. Hyacinthe, Quebec. It was considered to be their masterpiece with five manuals, one hundred and eleven speaking stops and nearly eight thousand pipes. Over five hundred miles of wires were used in its construction.

The carillon is another of Metropolitan's masterpieces. It was the first harmonically tuned instrument to be installed in North America. At present is has fifty-four bells, the largest one weighing four and a half tons.

The Metropolitan Silver Band, organized in 1934, has continued to give inspiration and pleasure at the church and elsewhere in the province. The choir also plays an important part in the worship services, as well as performing in outstanding programmes of choral music every year. Metropolitan Church is a centre of inspirational worship, consecrated leadership and constructive social service.

As with many other old churches in downtown Toronto in the 1960's, Metropolitan went through a period of discouragement as the diminishing congregation struggled to maintain services. But the remaining loyal members were determined that the church would survive. They dug in their heels and it did survive. Now a spirit of optimism prevails and the future looks promising.

Back in the 1960's the grounds south of the main door were made a public park maintained by the city. Since 1978, the church has conducted a program, "Summer in the Park", from the middle of June to the end of August, which provides entertainment, games, carillon recitals and friendliness for all those who use the park. Classical concerts are held in the church and guides conduct tours of this magnificent House of God that was designated as an historical site in 1975 by the Ontario Heritage Foundation.

St. Andrew's Presbyterian Church

TORONTO

St. Andrew's Presbyterian Church was begun in 1874 to serve a Church of Scotland congregation organized in 1830. Constructed largely of Georgetown sandstone, it was an outstanding example of Romanesque Revival architecture. The style was associated with medieval architecture in Scotland and the distinctively Scottish flank tower turrets further emphasized that significant connection.

Located in the heart of Toronto, St. Andrew's was dedicated in 1876. The corner of King and Simcoe Streets was a busy place even in those days and most of the congregation lived within walking distance of the church. Across the corner stood Government House. Upper Canada College occupied the second corner and on a third was a popular tavern. With St. Andrew's, the four corners were known locally as Legislation, Education, Damnation and Salvation.

St. Andrew's very early made changes in the old order of Presbyterian services by introducing instrumental music and by allowing the choir to wear robes. As early as the 1880's, it established the first Social Institute in Canada by conducting educational work among the new immigrants and urban poor, as well as giving needy children a chance to escape the summer heat of the city.

The building is massive and beautiful with its ornate furnishing, carved pews and tiled floor. The balcony, extending along both sides and around the back, is supported by fourteen slender pillars which appear to be hand-carved in a spiral design decorated with small balls and diamonds made of wood. The railing also appears hand-carved. Both pillars and railings are cast iron.

Twelve tall magnificent stained glass windows adorn each side of the sanctuary. One of them, the Highlanders Memorial Window, is especially significant. It was a gift from a member of the congregation to commemorate the famous 48th Highlanders of Canada, a regiment which was born in St. Andrew's Church.

By the middle of the 1900's, survival had become doubtful for the congregation. As with many other downtown churches, increasing numbers of people were moving out to the suburbs and the downtown core was being inundated by offices and warehouses. The congregation considered many times leaving the area

St. Andrew's Presbyterian Church in downtown Toronto stands on one of the four corners once known locally as Legislation, Education, Damnation and Salvation.

143

but, instead, hung on even though the building was beginning to need much restoration.

One of St. Andrew's many staunch supporters was Lieutenant Colonel The Honourable J. Keiller Mackay, D.S.O., K.Sc.J., V.D., L.L.D., D.C.L., G.C.L.J. He was an elder from 1931-1970, Justice of the Supreme Court of Ontario from 1925-1957, and Lieutenant Governor of Ontario from 1957-1963.

When the Rose Corporation first approached St. Andrew's congregation about buying the land surrounding the church, the congregation hesitated. After much deliberation they finally agreed to sell for two reasons. The first was that the Corporation agreed to build a place on the land architecturally compatible with the church. The second was that they needed the money to continue their social work as well as to pay off a debt and do some of the much-needed restoration.* In due time, Symphony Place, a 25-storey structure containing eighty-seven luxurious condominium residences was built. The Rose Corporation is the only downtown developer to take the time, money and effort to not only preserve an historical building but to enhance its beauty by complimenting the new with the old.

The restoration campaign to mark the 150th anniversary of the congregation is now almost complete. St. Andrew's in all its glory is a thriving, growing, caring church, continuing its tradition of funding social ministries to the disadvantaged of the city.

In 1983, a Karl Wilhelm tracker organ was installed. It is considered by many to be one of the finest instruments in North America and is featured in St. Andrew's annual concert series.

Today this busier than ever corner of King and Simcoe Streets is striking proof that by joining together texture, colour and lines, contemporary architecture can successfully harmonize with period architecture.

Standing in its original setting but now among the towering skyscrapers of Toronto, St. Andrew's values its rich history and celebrates its future.

---

*It was the congregation's idea and they decided to develop the land; the Rose Corporation submitted the plans most suitable.

THE KIEVER SYNAGOGUE

TORONTO

Situated in the Kensington Market district of Toronto, the Kiever Synagogue is one of the oldest synagogues in the city.

The congregation began as early as 1913, when a small group of people met for worship in each other's homes. By 1917, they were meeting in rented quarters. As their numbers continued to increase they were financially able to buy some of the surrounding property and, in 1923, the Kiever Synagogue was under construction. It opened for worship in 1927. Rabbi Solomon Langner officiated and remained in that capacity until 1974, after almost half a century of service.

Money was scarce in those days. Out of necessity the people did only what they could afford with the result that the building closely resembled a large square box surmounted by four domes, one on each of three corners and one in the center.

The basement floor was constructed of boards laid directly on the earth. Its one room was used as a chapel as well as for social gatherings. It was damp, cold, and uncomfortable and, over the years, the wood began to rot and the building became infested with termites. The outside walls were of double brick so there was no way they could be insulated against the cold.

The basement may not have been a thing of beauty but the sanctuary upstairs made up for it. The original doors were solid oak. Benches with open backs and turned legs were used in the beginning, having been brought from other houses, but have since been replaced with benches having solid backs. The Ark, also of oak, boasted hand-carved lions. The Scrolls (or Torah) kept within it were hand-written on parchment and covered with satin or velvet. The stained glass windows of Belgian glass were expensive, as far as the congregation was concerned, but actually were the cheapest they could find at the time.

During the Depression years, there was only enough money for basic repairs and painting. One man, a destitute painter too proud to ask for help, was given the job of decorating the walls in return for money. His paintings were done directly on the plastered walls. Since then, the years have taken their toll and very little evidence of them is left.

The restored Kiever Synagogue in the Kensington Market district of Toronto was the first synagogue in Ontario designated an historic site by the Toronto Historical Board.

During the 1950's and 1960's, the downtown area of Toronto changed radically when many families moved away to newer less-crowded parts of the city. Many old buildings were vandalized, among them the Kiever Synagogue. By the 1970's, in need of restoration and with no funds available, the congregation considered selling it. However, because the synagogue is one of the few of its type and had not been altered from its original form, the Toronto Jewish Congress Archives wanted to preserve it as an educational tool in the downtown area. They raised a considerable sum of money with difficulty but, with the help of a grant from Wintario and other private donations, restoration was finally begun.

The priceless stained glass windows had been smashed and could not be restored but the fragments were painstakingly gathered up and placed together until the original patterns could be distinguished. The windows were then duplicated by a Toronto Company with new stained glass. Plexiglass protectors were added on the outside to prevent further damage. The original oak doors had been destroyed and replaced with plywood. Two sets of beautiful new oak doors were installed and are reached by two stairways facing each other at the front entrance to the synagogue. A new roof was put on and the domes were repaired and painted blue and white. Much of the cosmetic work was done by volunteers.

The exterior of the building was sandblasted, showing to greater advantage the intricate design of brickwork just below the roof. The final restoration is not perfect but the survival of the building is guaranteed.

The original Ark and brasswork were saved and are in use today. The gallery extends around three sides of the sanctuary and it is there that the women sit during the service. In an Orthodox congregation the men occupy the main floor. They feel that this custom enables the people to concentrate better than if the men and women were sitting together.

The Kiever Synagogue, or to give it its proper name, Rodfei Shalom Anshei Kiev, which means Pursuers of Peace, Men of Kiev, was designated on May 14, 1979 an historic site by the Toronto

Historical Board under the Ontario Heritage Act. It was the first synagogue in Ontario to be so designated.

This fine old building sits across from a small park, a rather tranquil setting in such a crowded area of old homes packed closely together along a narrow street. It is a fitting tribute to the Jewish community who were so determined to keep alive that part of their heritage in Toronto's inner city.

St. John's United Church

ALLISTON

A great many of Ontario's old churches came into being through the efforts of the Wesleyan Methodists. They usually started out by worshipping in a small frame church and progressed until they were able to build something more permanent. St. John's United Church in Alliston is a prime example. This beautiful old church was built in 1872.

At that time, it was the largest church in Simcoe County, sixty-six feet long and forty-five feet wide, built in Gothic style with a tower and spire one hundred and thirty feet high. There was a gallery in the front end ornamented with gilt moulding. The entire cost of the church and sheds was less than seven thousand dollars. It is ironic to note from church records that George Shepherd hauled the first load for the construction of the new building; John Faithful laid the first brick and William Patience carried the hod for him. Thus Faithful and Patience are built into the structure.

Alliston had a disastrous fire in 1891 (May 8) when most of the business section of town was destroyed. Miraculously the church was spared by a change in the direction of the wind. Several years later, the spire was damaged by lightning and, in 1948, the wooden steeple broke off at the junction of the wood and brick of the tower during an eighty mile an hour gale.

In those early days worshippers arrived by horse and carriage or sleigh. A two hundred foot long driving shed was built to accommodate them. A list of rules was posted: 1) This is not a free shed but is for members and adherents of the church; 2) No one is permitted to feed his horse in this shed; 3) Tie your horse short; 4) Post no bills. The shed was later sold to Diamond Wood Products for five hundred and fifty dollars. It has since been demolished and the site is now used as a parking lot.

Well-kept records also tell us about the caretaking of the church. The following is a list of the caretaker's (sexton's) duties in 1891:

1. Look after the inside of the building and keep it clean by sweeping and dusting.

The caretaking records of the beautiful old St. John's United Church in Alliston will give you a few chuckles. How times have changed!

2. Build fires when necessary and keep the place sufficiently warm.

3. Build fires and heat water for cleaning.

4. Open the building and yard early, half hour before meetings.

5. Ring the bell for five minutes at each of the following times: Sundays, 10:00 and 10:25 a.m., 2:10, 6:00 and 6:25 p.m.; Wednesdays, 7:00 p.m. in winter and 7:30 p.m. in summer and for special services the same as on Wednesdays.

6. Turn on the light before and after meetings and keep all doors locked when building not in use.

7. Look after yards and shed and keep them clean. Clear snow from walks and driveways.

8. The above-mentioned meetings include church services, Sunday School, special meetings, funerals, lectures, concerts, tea meetings and committee meetings.

For the duties described, the caretaker received the sum of $5.00 per month. There were several applicants for the job. In 1920, other duties were added which included scrubbing the Sunday School room floor in May and November, cut the grass, keep the newly-installed "closet" thoroughly clean and supplied with paper, remove ashes, clean stovepipes and chimney and see that no disturbances occur at the time of services. Then, in 1928, the church was to be scrubbed at least twice a year. It is hoped that a pay increase was also added when the duties were. How times have changed!

The Sunday School room was used for special events in the town of Alliston as well as for Sunday School. The town Council used it in 1928 for a banquet to honour Mr. T.P. Loblaw, head of the grocery chain, for his most generous gift of a hospital for Alliston and the surrounding neighbourhood. This facility became a nursing home but was demolished in the 70's.

When an individual communion set was purchased in 1909, a contribution of $3.00 was made to the Barbara Heck Memorial Fund which originated in the Blue Church written about earlier.

The late Sir Frederick Banting, co-discoverer with Dr. Charles Best of insulin, was closely associated with this church. The Banting home, a short drive north of the town, is still occupied by members of the Banting family When this man, who did so much for diabetes sufferers, died in 1941, a Memorial Service was held in St. John's Church.

As with all the beautiful old churches in the small towns of Ontario, the building of them was a great achievement and represented sacrifice and devotion. Times have changed but these historic places of worship still stand for the same principles they started with, and all succeeding generations are the beneficiaries.

PARIS PLAINS & ST. JAMES

WESLEYAN METHODIST & ANGLICAN ❧ PARIS

The picturesque town of Paris and the surrounding area, the County of Brant, has an outstanding history of pioneer life. The site where the Nith and Grand Rivers meet was first settled in 1828 by Hiram Capron who chose to call it the "Forks of the Grand". Inspired by the many "plaster of Paris" deposits along the river Grand, the settlement was renamed Paris in 1831. Before even a school or church existed, Methodist itinerant preachers rode from Long Point on Lake Erie to Brantford, Paris, Galt and Copetown. The trip from station to station would be made in four weeks under favourable conditions but this could seldom be depended upon. In Spring and Fall, the swamps were almost impassable, the weary horses sometimes sinking to their knees at every step. In summer, swarms of mosquitoes made life nearly unbearable for horse and rider and, in winter, snow blocked the way.

The first meetings conducted by those preachers were held from settler's shack to settler's shack. In 1829, they were moved to the adjacent one room Maus School. When the old school was no longer needed, it was used as a Pioneer Museum for a time but is now made use of only occasionally as a community meeting place. Finally, in 1845, a little cobblestone church was built and dedicated as the West Dumfries Chapel.

Standing two miles north of Paris off Highway 24A that winds in graceful curves following an old Indian trail, this rare old church typifies the historic past of the area. The early pioneers gave their labour as a free offering and constructed their house of worship from the cobblestones taken from their farms and road-sides and some from the river bed itself. They built into it some-thing of their own sturdy characters and today, known as the Paris Plains Church, it is one of the best specimens of its kind to be found in this country.

The Plains from which the church derives its name consist of a rich level stretch of farming country running for many miles north of the Grand River. Conditions here were extremely attrac-tive to the pioneer farmers who settled the area early in the 19th century. The church building is of unusual architectural interest since it employs a comparatively rare type of cobblestone construc-

The unique Paris Plains Church was constructed from the cobblestones taken from the farms of the pioneers and from nearby roadsides and river beds.

tion. This method of building had been introduced into the Paris area by Levi Boughton, who emigrated to the district from Rochester, New York, in the late 1830's.

From the surrounding fields the members of the congregation gathered even, oval stones which were laid in level "courses" to build the walls. These stones were "sized" through a round ring to ensure uniform shape and contour. This method is believed to have been introduced to southern England by the Romans and brought to North America by unknown masons in the 19th century.

After the coming of the automobile, the church fell into disuse except as a Sunday School. In time vandals severely damaged the structure and a movement was on foot to have it torn down. There were, however, enough interested people who wanted the building preserved. A committee was formed, money was raised, and restoration began.

St. James Anglican, another cobblestone church in Paris, also has an outstanding history.

The Township of South Dumfries purchased the church and school from the Brant County Board of Education after the amalgamation of schools. The Township helps with some of the repairs and the committee raised the rest of the money needed. The church is not used on a regular basis but there is an annual service held in the summer.

The adjacent Maus Cemetery tells the story of countless pioneer families in the weathered tombstones. Early death visited many of those pioneers following the severe cold and plague. One stone dates back to the year 1833.

It is hoped that the generations of today and tomorrow will appreciate the unique landmark of a Pioneer Church, Cemetery and Pioneer School parcelled neatly together in a charming setting on one of Ontario's peaceful country roads.

Another of the early cobblestone churches lies in the heart of the town of Paris. It was built in 1839, a few years before the Paris Plains Church. A sum of money for its construction came from St. James Church, Edinburgh, Scotland, and from the Duchess of Leeds and the Paris church was given the same name, St. James. The cobblestones were obtained from the hill overlooking Willow Street, Paris, and were laid in the wall crosswise with the ends pointed outwards.

The Rev. William Morse became St. James' first minister. An accomplished musician, he brought the parts of a pipe organ from England and installed it in the dining room of his home where he also conducted a private school.

Before coming to St. James, Rev. Morse had been, in 1832, licensed as a Missionary Minister to the Diocese of Calcutta, India, and, in 1836, for Jamaica.

There is a story that St. James, at one time, had a "leper's pew". It may be just a story as there is no record of this anywhere but there is a low, Gothic-shaped door, now sealed off, in the original basement wall of the church. Owing to the fact that Rev. Morse was a missionary in India where leprosy was rampant, is it not possible that when he came to St. James, he would have a leper's pew installed? We will never know for sure whether that small doorway was where the lepers were led in to be unseen by the rest of the congregation.

Since its beginning, the church has undergone many changes. The original arched ceiling with oak beams was changed to the flat plastered ceiling of today and the gallery was removed, being described as unsightly. The exterior remains basically the same except for the addition of a modern education building and up-to-date kitchen, office, etc.

In 1910, a unique gift was received from a parishioner as a memorial. It consisted of a brass pulpit, reading desk and a chancel screen running across the width of the church. An original idea of the donor and the first of its kind, the brass tubing connecting the parts of the memorial was inset with miniature bulbs which were frosted, and produced a subdued light.

When the church celebrated its 125th Anniversary in 1964, a thank offering was raised under the name of "Return the Founding Grant". The idea was to "return" the grant that was given by St. James Church, Edinburgh, in 1839, by raising a like amount to assist with the building of a church in a modern pioneer setting. Eight hundred and twenty-five dollars was raised and the money was given towards the construction of the nave of St. Philip the Deacon Church in Lusaka, Zambia. The Edinburgh Church was informed that the Founding Grant had been returned.

The cobblestone churches of the Paris area are unique not only in Ontario but in all of Canada. Since their beginnings, succeeding congregations have seen to it that they have been restored and preserved for future generations as memorials to our pioneer ancestors.

KNESSETH ISRAEL SYNAGOGUE

TORONTO

West Toronto, since the arrival of the Grand Trunk Railway and the early days of the Stockyards at Keele and St. Clair, has always been a working class district. The Junction and in particular Maria Street, was home to many different ethnic groups including a sizeable population of Jews, some of whom had emigrated from Russia.

Jewish residents contributed greatly to local commerce through their involvement with many successful business enterprises, mostly modest retail operations. Bakers, tailors, furriers and druggists served The Junction well, as did family-operated appliance and paint and wallpaper stores.

Though businessmen and tradesmen by vocation, these same gentlemen were devoted scholars who gave of their limited free time to religious study and to the support of the Knesseth Israel Synagogue, known locally as "The Junction Schule."

The Synagogue was designed by architects Ellis and Connery and built in 1911 at 56 Maria Street.

Built of red brick with limestone dressings; the windows are distinguished by stone lintels and rock-faced sills. The cornerstones have projecting brick patterned aprons. Below arched gable parapets, three similar facades feature central wheel windows each with eighteen segments representing Life (Chai). A double flight of steps leads up to the main entrance on the west facade. The lower "shule" area is serviced by it's own side entrance.

The interior is traditional in plan with fine carved oak woodwork in the central Bima and Gallery railing. The oak fitments and wall paintings have special religious meaning and quality in craftsmanship.

The original owner of the Knesseth Israel Synagogue was a Board of Trustees made up of members of the congregation. As the

Knesseth Israel, one of West Toronto's landmarks is the oldest synagogue building still in use as a synagogue in Toronto.

159

city grew and the neighbourhood changed, many of the Jewish families moved elsewhere, thus diminishing the attendance as well as the financial support. However, the synagogue survived and some of its former members still come back to worship in the place where they grew up and received their first religious training.

On January 15, 1984, the Ontario Heritage Act authorized Toronto City Council to pass a by-law which designated the Knesseth Israel Synagogue as a property of architectural value and historic interest.

In the spring of that year, the unveiling of the Toronto Historical Board Plaque was an exciting event for the community. Dignitaries, well-known businessmen, members and friends came from all over. After a brief ceremony inside and the unveiling, they gathered in the back yard for a garden party to celebrate and renew old acquaintances. A roll call of former residents, some of whom may have been in attendance would include such family names as Fein, Silverman, Waisberg, Kirshenbaum, Shoom, Yankele, Tanenbaum, Goldstein, Osheroff, Mandel, Kronis, Alspector, Dubross, Krofchick, Greenblatt, Haberman, Raitblass, and Nikolaevsky. One oldtimer, Joseph Alexandroff, who had travelled some distance to attend, reminisced about the good old days in the Junction Schule.

Credit must be given to the many men and women, most of whom no longer reside in the area, who still maintain and contribute to Knesseth Israel in order that this, the oldest surviving synagogue building in Toronto still used as a synagugue, will be preserved for future generations.

JA'FFARI
ISLAMIC CENTRE

THORNHILL

Islam is not only a religion. It is a way of life. It is one of the three monotheistic religions in the world. Brought to this country by the Muslims, it is thought to be a recent addition. In fact, the recorded presence of Muslims in Canada dates back to the mid 19th century. The people immigrated from Syria, Albania, Yugoslavia and Turkey and, for the most part, settled in Western Canada.

A few Muslims came to Ontario but it wasn't until after the second world War that the numbers increased appreciably. By the mid 1960's to the mid 1970's the numbers grew considerably with immigrants arriving from Pakistan, Iraq, Iran, Uganda and other East Asian countries. At the present time, Ontario has the greatest concentration of Muslims in Canada.

The establishment of religious institutions has always been a priority of Muslims. The mosques, as they are called, are found in most Canadian cities. In the beginning, the people acquired old church buildings and converted them into mosques. More recently they have been in a position to build their own. The first mosque in Canada was built in Edmonton, Alberta, in 1938 but the first to be built in Metro Toronto, the Ja'Ffari Islamic Centre, opened in 1979.

Ja'Ffari Islamic Centre shares a parking lot with its next door neighbour, the Temple Har Zion, a fine example of neighbourly cooperation in these times of Middle East unrest.

The Centre is an impressive building from the outside. Its white dome towers among stately trees in a park-like setting. As you enter the main door, there is a vestibule where all shoes are removed and left. On the other side of double doors, you will find the large carpeted lecture hall. The first thing that takes your attention is the absence of chairs or pews and there is no sign of any musical instruments.

An archway at one end of the hall leads into the prayer hall. A sign over the arch reads: The plight of the Iraqi children should be everyone's concern. Please dig deep into your pockets.

At each side of the archway there is a calligraphed panel approximately ten by thirty feet in size. The right panel contains many verses from the Muslim scripture called the Qur'an and is written in Arabic. The panel on the left contains the sayings of the prophet Muhammad, the last message of Islam. The original art work was done on paper and was six months in the making.

The beautiful stained glass windows are also designed using Arabic letters and symbols. At the top of each is the Arabic word for God, "Allah".

Worshipers kneel on the rug in the mosque and the lecture room for prayers facing Mecca whereas, for lectures, the leader speaks from a pulpit made up of five steps so as to be seen by everyone. There are no ministers or priests, just scholars or laymen. When prostrate, the worshippers rest their foreheads on small round clay discs made from any clay but preferably that from the Holy Land. Strings of prayer beads are also used in the ritual. In mosques where the membership is small, individual prayer rugs may be used. Ja'Ffari has so many people at prayer that there may not be enough space available or practical for the individual rugs.

The Centre is a busy place every day of the week. There are specific times for prayer, Sunday School, meetings, etc. On Saturday and Sunday mornings, volunteers hold religious education classes for children where they are taught the principles of Islam. As well, Persian children who have grown up in Canada are taught the language of their mother country.

Some time ago a group called "Mosaic" met regularly to exchange ideas and customs. It was made up of representatives from all denominations in the area, Roman Catholic, Jewish, United Church, Anglican, Lutheran, Buddhists, Hindus, etc., a truly ecumenical gathering. The regular meetings dwindled after a while but the group tries to get together once a year for a "Peace Meal". Each member brings some food with the stipulation that everything must be vegetarian. This does not offend any denomination. The smaller group still meets infrequently.

One of the rooms in the basement of the mosque is a special room. When a member dies, the body is washed and prepared for burial in this room. No embalming is done and funeral homes are used to the minimal in accordance with the Islam custom.

Islam is a religion of peace — peace within one's self and peace with others. Unfortunately, because of the Middle Eastern events of the last three decasdes, Islam has often been branded by the media as a religion of violence. It is most unfair to blame the religion of Islam for the wrong-doings of some who call themselves Muslims.

The Temple Har Zion, a Jewish Synagogue next door, and the Ja'Ffari Islamic Centre share parking lots when necessary and are on very friendly terms with each other. It is refreshing to find such an arrangement in this time of such crisis in the Middle East. People the world over can learn a valuable lesson in brotherly love from these two different and distinct houses of worship.

St. Andrew's & The Ruins of St. Raphael

UNITED & ROMAN CATHOLIC

⚕ WILLIAMSTOWN

The far eastern counties of Ontario abound in historic build-ings. One such is St. Andrew's United Church in the village of Williamstown in Glengarry County.

As early as 1784, Sir John Johnson and his Loyalists from the Mohawk Valley in New York settled there. Then, in 1787, a group of Presbyterians, probably immigrants from Scotland, arrived, or-ganized a congregation and erected a log church. They replaced it in 1806 with a stone structure and, in that same year, a bell was pre-sented to the church by Sir Alexander Mackenzie, the great west-ern explorer. The present beautiful stone church, which became part of the United Church in 1925, was begun in 1812. Some years later, special pews were allotted to Mackenzie and other partners of the North West Exploration.

A small plaque on the gate regarding the adjacent cemetery admonishes visitors to "Tread softly, stranger, reverently draw near, the vanguard of a nation slumbers here".

In 1786, a group of some five hundred Scottish Highlanders who were Roman Catholics settled in the area near Williamstown. Under the leadership of Father Alexander (Scotus) Macdonell, they built a small church known as the "Blue Chapel" and dedicated it and the settlement to their Archangel Saint Raphael.

In 1815, a much larger church was begun to replace the little chapel. Father Macdonell, now Bishop Macdonell, and Archibald Fraser, a stone mason from Scotland, supervised the construction, built partly by subscription and partly by volunteer work. Stone from local quarries was carried by stoneboat in summer and sleigh in winter. The interior was constructed without pillars. Instead of nails, the men fashioned hardwood pegs by hand and used intricate wood joining methods. The church was completed and blessed in 1821 as the Church of St. Raphael.

Bishop Alexander Macdonell, one of the outstanding religious and political figures of the day, was the first Roman Catholic Bishop of Upper Canada and later a member of the Legislative Council of the Province of Ontario. Under his direction, the last large-scale emigration from the Scottish Highlands to the parish of

The Ruins of St. Raphael are all that is left of a once grand old church. The walls still stand just as the faith of our forefathers has stood down through the years.

St. Raphael took place in 1804. The Bishop had a mill constructed on the Garry River a few miles away to meet the needs of the parishioners. The settlement there became known as Priest's Mill and was later named Alexandria in honour of the bishop. The mill has since been made into a charming restaurant called The Priest's Mill which has several rooms for breakfast, lunch or dinner. The formal dining room, the Bishop Alex Room, is dedicated to the man who helped establish the first mill there and who was the first pastor of St. Raphael's Church.

For one hundred and fifty years the beautiful old church, with a seating capacity of one thousand, was the focal point of the parish. Three bells were donated to St. Raphael's. The large bell was named "Alexander", the medium bell was "Mary" and the small bell was given the name "Dionisius". The bells were brought from West Troy, New York, and were blessed by Bishop C.J. Phelan of Kingston on June 17, 1859.

Disaster struck on the evening of August 10, 1970, when flames destroyed the interior of St. Raphael's Church, leaving only the outside walls standing. For the remaining one hundred and fifty families in the parish, rebuilding the church to its former size and grandeur was impossible. A new smaller church, built on the west side of the Ruins, was opened in 1973.

The Ontario Heritage Foundation agreed to stabilize the remaining walls of the church as "Ruins" in 1974 and a plaque was erected at the site. Another plaque near it was placed there by the Historic Sites and Monuments Board of Canada and describes the life and work of Bishop Alexander Macdonell.

The Ruins of St. Raphael are an impressive sight. The walls, approximately three feet thick, straight and sturdy, are encrusted with moss and lichen in many places. As you go through the open front entrance you are awed by the size of the building which appears to have been built in the style of the Latin Cross. Just inside the door, displayed on a round concrete block is the largest of the bells, the Alexander, nearly half of it having been melted away in the disastrous fire. The words MENEELY'S, WEST TROY, N.Y. 1859, are still visible near the top of the bell.

The acres of cemetery surrounding the Ruins are well maintained. The names on the tombstones, Cameron, Mackenzie, MacMillan, Frobisher, McTavish, McGillvray, McDonell, Fraser, Thompson, McLellan, Fairbairn, Kennedy, McPhail, etc. speak of the Scottish heritage of the area. Tombstones date back as early as 1827, some of them so old that the names and dates are completely obliterated.

The Ruins of St. Raphael, tall and stark on the hill overlooking this beautiful part of Ontario, have a story to tell to all who stop to look. They tell of the strong and steadfast faith of the pioneers who built the church. Succeeding generations have benefitted from their labours and, like the stone walls of the Ruins, their faith will stand.

POSTSCRIPT

The places of worship written about in this book are just a selected sampling of the many unique old religious buildings within Ontario.

Many more are hidden away in downtown areas of big cities, in small towns or on country roads. Some have been completely neglected and abused and stand forlornly decorated with rodents' nests, cobwebs and broken windows. Others have been turned into private homes, restaurants, antique shops, flea markets or hand-crafted gift boutiques. Lodges, Senior Citizen groups or youth organizations have made some into useful community meeting places. A few are used as storage sheds for grain or old furniture.

Whatever their present use or condition, they were, in the beginning, built with the faith of our forefathers and remain forever reminders of the dedication of the pioneers to a way of life, trusting in a benevolent God for all their needs.

SUGGESTED READING

The Polish People in Canada – A Visual History by William Makowski, Tundra Books, 1987

The Known and the Unknown – Harriet Beecher Stowe by Edward Wagenknecht, New York University Press, 1965

The Wheel of Things, A Biography of Lucy Maud Montgomery by Mollie Gillen, Fitzhenry & Whiteside, 1975

Florence Nightingale 1820–1910 by Cecil Woodham-Smith, Constable & Company, Ltd. London, England, 1950

Eminent Victorians Collected works of Lytton Strachey, Chatto & Windus, London, England, 1960

The Great Canadian Road – A History of Yonge Street by Jay Myers, Red Rock Publishing Co. Ltd. Toronto, 1977

Separate and Peculiar by Isaac Horst, 1979

Firm Foundations – A Chronicle of Toronto's Metropolitan United Church and Her Methodist Origins, 1795–1984 by Judith St. John, Metropolitan United Church, 1988

Religion in Canadian Society Edited by Stewart Crysdale & Les Wheatcraft, Macmillan of Canada, 1976

Chronicles of Canada: a. *The Jesuit Missions* by Thomas Guthrie Marquis b. *The United Empire Loyalists* by W. Stewart Wallace c. *Pathfinders of the Great Plains* by Lawrence J. Burpee d. *The War Chief of the Six Nations* by Louis Aubrey Wood University of Toronto Press, 1964

New Oswegatchie by Edwin A. Livingston C.D., U.E. Genealogist, specializing in United Empire Loyalist Research

Bishop Alexander Macdonell and the Politics of Upper Canada by James Edgar Rea Toronto, Ontario Historical Society, 1974

BIBLIOGRAPHY

McGibbon, V.R., *Ottawa Valley Village 1823–1860*, Pakenham

MacFarlane, Corinne, for the Women's Auxiliary, *The History of St. Peter Celestine Church*, 1977

Makowski, William, *The Polish People in Canada, A Visual History*, Tundra Books, 1987

Broadbridge, Arthur, *The History of the Church of St. Peter*, Cobourg

Committee, The, *The Parish Church of St. Luke, Sesquicentennial, 1834–1984*, 1984

Zimmerman, the late Canon W.J., *Chapel Notes and The Story of the Windows*, 1965

Phelps, Arthur D., *The Life of Josiah Henson as narrated by Himself*, Boston,U.S.A.,   1849
Reproduced by Uncle Tom's Cabin Museum, Dresden, 1965

Chapple, William, *The Story of Uncle Tom*, Uncle Tom's Cabin Museum, Dresden

Mustard, Margaret, and Clarke, Wilde, *L.M. Montgomery as Mrs. Ewan Macdonald*, 1965

Gillen, Mollie, *The Wheel of Things— A Biography of Lucy Maud Montgomery*, Fitzhenry and Whiteside, 1975

Committee, The, *The Sesquicentennial of St. Paul's Anglican Church*, Uxbridge, 1984

Uxbridge Scott Historical Museum, *The Thomas Foster Memorial*, 1986

McIlwraith, Verne, *The Story of a Parish*, Guelph Historical Society, 1967

Collins, Rev. T., *The History of the Church of Our Lady Parish*, Guelph, 1989

Smiley, Barbara, *The History of St. John the Evangelist Anglican Church*, Rockwood, 1985

Duncan, Dorothy, *Black Creek Pioneer Village*, Metropolitan Toronto and Region Conservation Authority.

Scadding, Henry, *Toronto of Old, Collections and Recollections*, Toronto, 1873

Fraser, Alexander, *Sixteenth Report of the Department of Archives for the Province of Ontario, Land and Settlement in Upper Canada 1783–1840*, 1921

St. John, Judith, *A Chronicle of Toronto's Metropolitan United Church and Her Methodist Origins, 1795–1894*, Metropolitan United Church, 1988

Horst, Isaac, *Separate and Peculiar*, 1979

Committee, The, *The Centennial of St. John's United Church*, Alliston, 1972

Neilson, James G., *The 150th Anniversary Book of St. James Anglican Church*, Paris, 1989

Archives, United Church of Canada, *Church History Collection*, Toronto

Archives, *Diocese of Algoma*, Sault Ste. Marie

Myers, Jay, *The Great Canadian Road—A History of Yonge Street*, Red Rock Publishing Co. Ltd., 1977

ABOUT THE AUTHOR

Violet Holroyd, a native of Toronto, has spent over five years in the preparation of Foundations of Faith. She and husband, Gordon, travelled throughout Ontario to personally inspect historic centres of worship and interview local people. The author's interests include music, local history, and an active volunteer role with the James Shaver Woodsworth Foundation, Etobicoke.

Outside Back Cover: Photo shows Violet and Gordon Holroyd pinpointing a favourite destination on their much-used Ontario road map.